DIABETIC
AIR FRYER
COOKBOOK

1200-Day Easy and Delicious Recipes for Healthier and
More Energetic Living.
Take Care of Your Well-Being without Sacrificing Your
Favorite Flavors
+
30-Day Meal Plan

Karen Stevens

Table of Contents

Introduction

What Is An Air Fryer?

Air fryer is a kitchen appliance that uses hot air to cook food. It does not require oil to fry or cook your food. The air fryer is a much healthier cooking tool to fry foods like potatoes and other root vegetables. The air fryer cooks with about 80% less saturated fat than your standard deep fryer or skillet.

You might find some difficulty in understanding how the air fryer works, but once you see it cook a potato in a bowl of fat-free oil, you'll understand exactly how the process works.

Apart from frying, air fryers are great for roasting and baking. It's also great for preparing fries, pizza, croquettes and so on. There are no extra oil usage and it releases less grease compared to regular oven or deep fryer.

They are more energy-efficient than the traditional ovens too, so you can have guilt-free yummy food anytime! Air fryer is one appliance that has many features in a single unit. These features or components make the use of an air fryer very easy, and controlling the temperature to perfectly cook your favorite food is a guarantee!

Most air fryers have a digital display screen. This makes it much easier for you to monitor how your food is cooked. It also has an inbuilt timer Function that helps you know how long you need to cook food. This timer means you won't have to over or undercook. Most air fryers come with wide temperature range from 120 to 540 °F that makes the cooking more flexible and healthier because the heat is distributed evenly throughout the food

How The Air Fryer Works

Air frying is a cooking method where food is cooked in an enclosed chamber through the circulation of hot air around the chamber. This cooking process locks in moisture and sears the outside of the food to give it a golden-brown color. It's also possible for foods to taste better when air-frying them, rather than using the usual method of deep frying.

Air Fryer Benefits For Diabetics

If you have diabetes, you know how essential it is to use an air fryer. It's a perfect way to cook foods that are low in carbohydrates and high in healthy fat. When you have diabetes, it can be tough to find healthy alternatives to traditional high-fat foods. Luckily, you don't have to surrender your best-loved foods as long as you have an air fryer.

Air frying is a way to cook with very little fat. You can use just about any food you like in this way. Foods such as chips, fries, vegetables, and meat are examples of foods that can be fried using an air fryer.

When you want food with great taste, using the right proportion of ingredients is essential. However, you must utilize the right tool to get the job done. With the diabetic cookbook air fryer, you can cook just about anything. Using the air fryer will also cook your food more healthier and faster than most other ways of cooking.

Food cooked in an air fryer will not be as oily as traditional oil frying. This is because the air fryer uses less oil than a conventional fryer. All the fat and oil in the food goes directly into the food, leaving no pockets of oil in your air fryer.

You can also make healthier whole foods with air fryers, unlike the traditional frying method. Often time, many people try to lose weight by replacing fried foods with steamed foods, which in most cases does not work. When you use the traditional, oil-fried chicken sandwich, it contains lots of calories and unhealthy fat that you have to eat with your sandwich. Using air fryers can help you eliminate the calories and fats, thereby making your sandwich yummy and healthier.

A typical air-fried chicken breast contains about 50% lesser calories than the same piece of fried chicken breast without any modifications to its cooking method. Likewise, vegetables cooked in an air fryer retain more water compared to boiled or steamed ones. That means air-fried vegetables are more nutritious and healthier for you since they contain lesser calories.

CHAPTER 1: Breakfasts

1. Spinach and Tomato Egg Cup

Preparation time: 5 minutes

Cooking time: 10 minutes

Servings: 1

Ingredients:

- 2 egg whites, beaten
- 2 tablespoons chopped tomato
- 2 tablespoons chopped spinach
- Pinch of kosher salt
- Red pepper flakes (optional)

Directions:

1. Spray a 3-inch ramekin with nonstick cooking spray, then combine the egg whites, tomato, spinach, kosher salt, and red pepper flakes (if using) in the ramekin.
2. Place the ramekin in the air fryer's basket and bake at 300 °F (149 °C) for 10 minutes or till the eggs are ready.
3. Remove the ramekin from the fryer and allow cooling on a wire rack for 5 minutes before serving.

Per serving: Calories: 32Kcal; Fat: 0g; Protein: 7g; Carbohydrates: 1g; Sugar: 1g; Sodium: 184mg

2. Egg Muffins with Bell Pepper

Preparation time: 5 minutes

Cooking time: 10 minutes

Servings: 2

Ingredients:

- 4 large eggs
- ½ bell pepper, finely chopped
- 1 tablespoon finely chopped red onion
- ¼ teaspoon kosher salt
- 2 tablespoons shredded Cheddar cheese
- ¼ teaspoon freshly ground black pepper and more for serving

Directions:

1. In a large bowl, whisk the eggs together, and then stir in the bell pepper, red onion, kosher salt, and black pepper.
2. Spray two 3-inch ramekins with nonstick cooking spray, then pour half the egg mixture into each ramekin and then place the ramekins in the fryer basket. Bake at 390 °F (199 °C) for 8 minutes.
3. Pause the fryer, sprinkle 1 tablespoon of shredded Cheddar cheese on each cup, and bake for 2 more minutes.
4. Remove the ramekins from the fryer and allow cooling on a wire rack for 5 minutes, then turn the omelet cups out on plates and sprinkle some black pepper on top before serving.

Per serving: Calories: 172Kcal; Fat: 12g; Protein: 14g; Carbohydrates: 2g; Sugar: 1g; Sodium: 333mg

3. Egg-in-a-Hole

Preparation time: 5 minutes

Cooking time: 5 to 7 minutes

Servings: 1

Ingredients:

- 1 slice whole grain bread
- 1 large egg
- ⅛ teaspoon kosher salt
- ¼ cup diced avocado
- ¼ cup diced tomato
- Pinch of freshly ground black pepper

Directions:

1. Spray your baking pan with nonstick cooking spray, and then use a ring mold or a sharp knife to cut a 3-inch hole in the center of the whole grain bread. Place the bread slice and the circle in the pan.

2. Crack the egg into the hole, then season with the kosher salt. Bake at 360 °F (182 °C) for 5 to 7 minutes or until the egg is cooked as desired.

3. Remove the pan from the fryer and allow to cool on a wire rack for 5 minutes before transferring the toast to a plate, then sprinkle the avocado, tomato, and black pepper on top before serving.

Per serving: Calories: 220Kcal; Fat: 12g; Protein: 10g; Carbohydrates: 18g; Sugar: 4g; Sodium: 406mg

4. Egg and Cheese Pockets

Preparation time: 10 minutes

Cooking time: 35 minutes

Servings: 4

Ingredients:

- 1 large egg, beaten
- Pinch of kosher salt
- ½ sheet puff pastry
- 1 slice Cheddar cheese, divided into 4 pieces

Directions:

1. Pour the egg into a baking pan, season with the kosher salt, and bake at 330 °F (166 °C) for 3 minutes. Pause the fryer, gently scramble the egg, and bake for 2 more minutes. Remove the egg from the fryer, keeping the fryer on and set the egg aside to slightly cool.

2. Roll the puff pastry out flat and divide into 4 pieces.

3. Place a piece of Cheddar cheese and ¼ of the egg on one side of a piece of pastry,

fold the pastry over the egg and cheese and use a fork to press the edges closed. Repeat this process with the remaining pieces.

4. Place 2 pockets in the fryer and bake for 15 minutes or until golden brown. Repeat this process with the other 2 pockets.

5. Remove the pockets from the fryer and allow to cool on a wire rack for 5 minutes before serving.

Per serving: Calories: 215Kcal; Fat: 15g; Protein: 6g; Carbohydrates: 14g; Sugar: 0g; Sodium: 143mg

5. Huevos Rancheros

Preparation time: 20 minutes

Cooking time: 25 minutes

Servings: 4

Ingredients:

- 4 large eggs
- ¼ teaspoon kosher salt
- ¼ cup masa harina (corn flour)
- 1 teaspoon olive oil
- ¼ cup warm water
- ½ cup salsa
- ¼ cup crumbled queso fresco or feta cheese

Directions:

1. Crack the eggs into a baking pan, season with the kosher salt, and bake at 330 °F (166 °C) for 3 minutes. Pause the fryer, gently scramble the eggs and bake for 2 more minutes. Remove the eggs from the fryer, keeping the fryer on and set the eggs aside to slightly cool. (Clean the baking pan before making the tortillas.)

2. Increase the temperature to 390 °F (199ºC).

3. In a medium bowl, combine the masa harina, olive oil, and ¼ teaspoon of kosher

salt by hand, then slowly pour in the water, stirring until a soft dough forms.

4. Divide the dough into 4 equal balls, then place each ball between 2 pieces of parchment paper and use a pie plate or a rolling pin to flatten the dough.

5. Spray the baking pan with nonstick cooking spray, then place one flattened tortilla in the pan and air fry for 5 minutes. Repeat this process with the remaining tortillas.

6. Remove the tortillas from the fryer and place on a serving plate, then top each tortilla with the scrambled eggs, salsa, and cheese before serving.

Per serving: Calories: 136Kcal; Fat: 8g; Protein: 8g; Carbohydrates: 8g; Sugar: 2g; Sodium: 333mg

6. Shrimp Rice Frittata

Preparation time: 15 minutes
Cooking time: 14 to 18 minutes
Servings: 4
Ingredients:

- 4 eggs
- Pinch salt
- ½ teaspoon dried basil
- Nonstick cooking spray
- ½ cup cooked rice
- ½ cup chopped cooked shrimp
- ½ cup baby spinach
- ½ cup grated Monterey Jack or Cojack cheese

Directions:

1. In a mini bowl, beat the eggs with the salt and basil until frothy. Spray your baking pan with nonstick cooking spray.

2. Combine the shrimp, rice, and spinach in your prepared pan. Pour the eggs in and sprinkle with the cheese.

3. Bake at 320 °F (160ºC) for 14 to 18 minutes or until the frittata is puffed and golden brown.

Per serving: Calories: 227Kcal; Fat: 9g; Protein: 16g; Carbohydrates: 19g; Sugar: 1g; Sodium: 232mg

7. Vegetable Frittata

Preparation time: 10 minutes
Cooking time: 8 to 12 minutes
Servings: 4
Ingredients:

- ½ cup chopped red bell pepper
- ⅓ cup minced onion
- ⅓ cup grated carrot
- 1 teaspoon olive oil
- 6 egg whites
- 1 egg
- ⅓ cup 2% milk
- 1 tablespoon grated Parmesan cheese

Directions:

1. In a baking pan, stir together the red bell pepper, onion, carrot, and olive oil. Put the pan into the air fryer. Bake at 350 °F (177 °C) for 4 to 6 minutes, shaking the basket once, until the vegetables are tender.

2. Meanwhile, in your medium bowl, beat the egg whites, egg, and milk until combined.

3. Pour the egg mixture over the vegetables in the pan. Sprinkle with the Parmesan cheese. Return the pan to the air fryer.

4. Bake for 4 to 6 minutes more, or until the frittata is puffy and set.

5. Cut into 4 wedges and serve.

Per serving: Calories: 78Kcal; Fat: 3g; Protein: 8g; Carbohydrates: 5g; Sugar: 3g; Sodium: 116mg

8. Egg and Avocado Breakfast Burrito

Preparation time: 10 minutes

Cooking time: 3 to 5 minutes

Servings: 4

Ingredients:

- 2 hard-boiled egg whites, chopped
- 1 hard-boiled egg, chopped
- 1 avocado, peeled, pitted, and chopped
- 1 red bell pepper, chopped
- 3 tablespoons low-sodium salsa, plus additional for serving (optional)
- 1 (1.2-ounce / 34-g) slice low-sodium, low-fat American cheese, torn into pieces
- 4 low-sodium whole-wheat flour tortillas

Directions:

1. In a medium bowl, thoroughly mix the egg whites, egg, avocado, red bell pepper, salsa, and cheese.
2. Place the tortillas on a work surface and evenly divide the filling among them. Fold in the edges and roll it up. Secure the burritos with toothpicks if necessary.
3. Put the burritos in the air fryer basket. Air fry at 390 °F (199 °C) for 3 to 5 minutes, or until the burritos are light golden brown and crisp. Serve with more salsa (as you prefer it).

Per serving: Calories: 205Kcal; Fat: 8g; Protein: 9g; Carbohydrates: 27g; Sugar: 1g; Sodium: 109mg.

9. Mixed Berry Dutch Pancake

Preparation time: 10 minutes

Cooking time: 12 to 16 minutes

Servings: 4

Ingredients:

- 2 egg whites
- 1 egg
- ½ cup whole-wheat pastry flour
- ½ cup 2% milk
- 1 teaspoon pure vanilla extract
- 1 tablespoon unsalted butter, melted
- 1 cup sliced fresh strawberries
- ½ cup fresh blueberries
- ½ cup fresh raspberries

Directions:

1. In a medium bowl, use an eggbeater or hand mixer to quickly mix the egg whites, egg, pastry flour, milk, and vanilla until well combined.
2. Use your pastry brush to oil your baking pan with the melted butter. Add the butter immediately and place the baking pan in the fryer. Bake at 330 °F (166 °C) for 12 to 16 minutes, or until the pancake is puffed and golden brown.
3. Remove the pan from your air fryer; the pancake will fall. Top with the strawberries, blueberries, and raspberries. Serve immediately.

Per serving: Calories: 155Kcal; Fat: 5g; Protein: 7g; Carbohydrates: 21g; Sugar: 6g; Sodium: 59mg

10. Crunchy Fried French Toast Sticks

Preparation time: 6 minutes
Cooking time: 10 to 14 minutes
Servings: 4
Ingredients:

- 3 slices low-sodium whole-wheat bread, each cut into 4 strips
- 1 tablespoon unsalted butter, melted
- 1 egg
- 1 egg white
- 1 tablespoon 2% milk
- 1 tablespoon honey
- 1 cup sliced fresh strawberries
- 1 tablespoon freshly squeezed lemon juice

Directions:

1. Place the bread strips on a plate and drizzle with the melted butter.
2. In your shallow bowl, beat the egg, egg white, milk, and honey.
3. Dip the bread into the egg mixture and place on a wire rack to let the batter drip off.
4. Air fry half of the bread strips at 380 °F (193 °C) for 5 to 7 minutes, turning the strips with tongs once during cooking, until golden brown. Repeat with the remaining strips.
5. In a small bowl, mash the strawberries and lemon juice with a fork or potato masher. Serve the strawberry sauce with the French toast sticks.

Per serving: Calories: 145Kcal; Fat: 5g; Protein: 7g; Carbohydrates: 18g; Sugar: 7g; Sodium: 120mg

11. Pumpkin Oatmeal with Raisins

Preparation time: 10 minutes
Cooking time: 10 minutes
Servings: 3
Ingredients:

- 1 cup rolled oats
- 2 tablespoons raisins
- ¼ teaspoon ground cinnamon
- Pinch of kosher salt
- ¼ cup pumpkin purée
- 2 tablespoons pure maple syrup
- 1 cup of low-fat milk

Directions:

1. In your medium bowl, combine the rolled oats, raisins, ground cinnamon, and kosher salt, then stir in the pumpkin purée, maple syrup, and low-fat milk.
2. Spray a baking pan with nonstick cooking spray, then pour the oatmeal mixture into the pan and bake at 300 °F (149 °C) for 10 minutes.
3. Remove the oatmeal from the fryer and allow to cool in the pan on a wire rack for 5 minutes before serving.

Per serving: Calories: 304Kcal; Fat: 4g; Protein: 10g; Carbohydrates: 57g; Sugar: 26g; Sodium: 140mg

12. Mushroom and Black Bean Burrito

Preparation time: 10 minutes
Cooking time: 15 minutes
Servings: 1
Ingredients:

- 2 tablespoons canned black beans, rinsed & drained

- ¼ cup sliced baby portobello mushrooms
- 1 teaspoon olive oil
- Pinch of kosher salt
- 1 large egg
- 1 slice low-fat Cheddar cheese
- 1 (8-inch) whole grain flour tortilla
- Hot sauce (optional)

Directions:

1. Spray your baking pan with nonstick cooking spray, then place the black beans and baby portobello mushrooms in the pan, drizzle with the olive oil, and season with the kosher salt.
2. Bake at 360 °F (182 °C) for 5 minutes, then pause the fryer to crack the egg on top of the beans and mushrooms. Bake for 8 more minutes or until the egg is cooked as desired.
3. Pause the fryer again, top the egg with cheese, and bake for 1 more minute.
4. Remove the pan from the fryer, then use a spatula to place the bean mixture on the whole grain flour tortilla. Fold in the sides and roll from front to back. Serve warm with the hot sauce on the side (if using).

Per serving: Calories: 276Kcal; Fat: 12g; Protein: 16g; Carbohydrates: 26g; Sugar: 2g; Sodium: 306mg

13. Bacon and Egg Sandwiches

Preparation time: 3 minutes

Cooking time: 8 minutes

Servings: 2

Ingredients:

- 2 large eggs
- ¼ teaspoon kosher salt, divided
- ¼ teaspoon freshly ground black pepper, divided (and extra for serving)
- 2 slices Canadian bacon

- 2 slices American cheese
- 2 whole grain English muffins, sliced in half

Directions:

1. Spray two ramekins measuring 3 inches in diameter with nonstick cooking spray, then crack an egg into each ramekin and add half of the kosher salt and half of the black pepper.
2. Place the ramekins in the fryer basket and bake them at 360 °Ffor 5 minutes.
3. 3. Stop the fryer and place a slice of Canadian bacon and a slice of American cheese on top of each egg that is partially cooked.
4. Continue baking for three minutes, or until the cheese has melted and the egg yolk is just set.
5. 5. Remove the ramekins from the fryer and allow them to cool for 2 to 3 minutes on a wire rack, then invert the eggs, bacon, and cheese onto English muffins and sprinkle with black pepper before serving.

Per serving: Calories: 309Kcal; Fat: 13g; Protein: 22g; Carbohydrates: 26g; Sugar: 3g; Sodium: 618mg

14. Almond Crunch Granola

Preparation time: 5 minutes

Cooking time: 8 to 10 minutes

Servings: 1

Ingredients:

- ⅔ cup rolled oats
- ⅓ cup unsweetened shredded coconut
- ⅓ cup sliced almonds
- 1 teaspoon canola oil
- 2 teaspoons honey
- ¼ teaspoon kosher salt

Directions:

1. In your medium bowl, combine the rolled oats, shredded coconut, sliced almonds, canola oil, honey, and kosher salt.

2. Place a small piece of parchment paper on the bottom of a baking pan, then pour the mixture into the pan then distribute it evenly. Bake at 360 °F (182 °C) for 5 minutes, pause the fryer to gently stir the granola, and bake for 3 more minutes.

3. Remove the granola from the fryer and allow it to cool for five minutes in the pan on a wire rack, then transfer the granola to a serving plate to cool completely before serving. (It becomes crunchier as it cools. Store the granola in your airtight container for up to 2 weeks.)

Per serving: Calories: 181Kcal; Fat: 9g; Protein: 4g; Carbohydrates: 21g; Sugar: 4g; Sodium: 94mg

15. Yogurt Raspberry Cake

Preparation time: 10 minutes

Cooking time: 8 minutes

Servings: 4

Ingredients:

- ½ cup whole wheat pastry flour
- ⅛ teaspoon kosher salt
- ¼ teaspoon baking powder
- ½ cup whole milk vanilla yogurt
- 2 tablespoons canola oil
- 2 tablespoons pure maple syrup
- ¾ cup fresh raspberries

Directions:

1. In a huge bowl, combine the whole wheat pastry flour, kosher salt, and baking powder, then stir in the whole milk vanilla yogurt, canola oil, and maple syrup and gently fold in the raspberries.

2. Spray a baking pan with nonstick cooking spray, then pour the cake batter into the

pan and bake at 300 °F (149 °C) for 8 minutes.

3. Remove the cake from the fryer and allow to cool in the pan on a wire rack for 10 mins. before cutting and serving.

Per serving: Calories: 168Kcal; Fat: 8g; Protein: 3g; Carbohydrates: 21g; Sugar: 8g; Sodium: 82mg

16. Scotch Eggs

Preparation time: 10 minutes

Cooking time: 15 minutes

Servings: 4

Ingredients:

- 1-pound pork sausage, pastured
- 2 tablespoons chopped parsley
- 1/8 teaspoon salt
- 1/8 teaspoon grated nutmeg
- 1 tablespoon chopped chives
- 1/8 teaspoon ground black pepper
- 2 teaspoons ground mustard, and more as needed
- 4 eggs, hard-boiled, shell peeled
- 1 cup shredded parmesan cheese, low-fat

Directions:

1. Switch on the air fryer, insert fryer basket, grease it with olive oil, then shut with its lid, set the fryer at 400 °F and preheat for 10 minutes.

2. Meanwhile, place sausage in a bowl, add salt, black pepper, parsley, chives, nutmeg, and mustard, then stir until well mixed and shape the mixture into four patties.

3. Peel each boiled egg, then place an egg on a patty and shape the meat around it until the egg has evenly covered.

4. Place cheese in a shallow dish and then roll the egg in the cheese until covered

completely with cheese; prepare remaining eggs in the same manner.

5. Then open the fryer, add eggs in it, close with its lid and cook for 15 minutes at 400 ºF until it is golden and crispy, turning the eggs and spraying with oil halfway through the frying.

6. When air fryer beeps, open its lid, transfer eggs onto a serving plate and serve with mustard.

Per serving: Calories: 533Kcal; Fat: 43g; Protein: 33g; Carbohydrates: 2g; Sugar: 1g; Sodium: 164mg

17. Spinach and Tomato Frittata

Preparation time: 5 minutes

Cooking time: 21 minutes

Servings: 4

Ingredients:

- 4 tablespoons chopped spinach
- 4 mushrooms, sliced
- 3 cherry tomatoes, halved
- 1 green onion, sliced
- 1 tablespoon chopped parsley
- ¾ teaspoon salt
- 1 tablespoon chopped rosemary
- 4 eggs, pastured
- 3 tablespoons heavy cream, reduced-fat
- 4 tablespoons grated cheddar cheese, reduced-fat

Directions:

1. Switch on the air fryer, insert fryer pan, grease it with olive oil, then shut with its lid, set the fryer at 350 °F and preheat for 5 minutes.

2. Meanwhile, crack eggs in a bowl, whisk in the cream until smooth, then add remaining ingredients and stir until well combined.

3. Then open the fryer, pour the frittata mixture in it, close with its lid and cook for 12 to 16 minutes until its top is golden, frittata has set, and inserted toothpick into the frittata slides out clean.

4. When air fryer beeps, open its lid, transfer frittata onto a serving plate, then cut into pieces and serve.

Per serving: Calories: 147Kcal; Fat: 11g; Protein: 9g; Carbohydrates: 3g; Sugar: 2g; Sodium: 182mg

18. Herb Frittata

Preparation time: 10 minutes

Cooking time: 25 minutes

Servings: 4

Ingredients:

- 2 tablespoons chopped green scallions
- 1/2 teaspoon ground black pepper
- 2 tablespoons chopped cilantro
- 1/2 teaspoon salt
- 2 tablespoons chopped parsley
- 1/2 cup half and half, reduced-fat
- 4 eggs, pastured
- 1/3 cup shredded cheddar cheese, reduced-fat

Directions:

1. Turn on the air fryer, place the fryer basket inside, coat it with olive oil, close the lid, set the temperature to 330 °F , and preheat for 10 minutes.

2. Meanwhile, take a round heatproof pan that fits into the fryer basket, grease it well with oil and set aside until required.

3. Crack the eggs in a bowl, beat in half-and-half, then add remaining ingredients, beat until well mixed and pour the mixture into prepared pan.

4. Open the fryer, place the pan in it, close with its lid and cook for 15 minutes at the 330 °F until its top is golden, frittata has set and inserted toothpick into the frittata slides out clean.

5. When air fryer beeps, open its lid, take out the pan, then transfer frittata onto a serving plate, cut it into pieces and serve.

Per serving: Calories: 141Kcal; Fat: 10g; Protein: 8g; Carbohydrates: 2g; Sugar: 2g; Sodium: 174mg

19. Pancakes

Preparation time: 5 minutes
Cooking time: 29 minutes
Servings: 4
Ingredients:

- 1 1/2 cup coconut flour
- 1 teaspoon salt
- 3 1/2 teaspoons baking powder
- 1 tablespoon erythritol sweetener
- 1 1/2 teaspoon baking soda
- 3 tablespoons melted butter
- 1 1/4 cups milk, unsweetened, reduced-fat
- 1 egg, pastured

Directions:

1. Turn on the air fryer, insert the fryer pan, coat it with olive oil, close the lid, set the temperature to 220 °F , and preheat for 5 minutes.

2. Meanwhile, take a medium bowl, add all the ingredients in it, whisk until well blended and then let the mixture rest for 5 minutes.

3. Open the fryer, pour in some of the pancake mixture as thin as possible, close with its lid and cook for 6 minutes until nicely golden, turning the pancake halfway through the frying.

4. When air fryer beeps, open its lid, transfer pancake onto a serving plate and use the remaining batter for cooking more pancakes in the same manner.

5. Serve straight away with fresh fruits slices.

Per serving: Calories: 237.7Kcal; Fat: 10.2g; Protein: 6.3g; Carbohydrates: 39.2g; Sugar: 3g; Sodium: 156mg

20. Zucchini Bread

Preparation time: 25 minutes
Cooking time: 40 minutes
Servings: 8
Ingredients:

- ¾ cup shredded zucchini
- 1/2 cup almond flour
- 1/4 teaspoon salt
- 1/4 cup cocoa powder, unsweetened
- 1/2 cup chocolate chips, unsweetened, divided
- 6 tablespoons erythritol sweetener
- 1/2 teaspoon baking soda
- 2 tablespoons olive oil
- 1/2 teaspoon vanilla extract, unsweetened
- 2 tablespoons butter, unsalted, melted
- 1 egg, pastured

Directions:

1. Turn on the air fryer, place the fryer basket inside, coat it with olive oil, close the lid, set the temperature to 310 °F , and preheat for 10 minutes.

2. Meanwhile, place flour in a bowl, add salt, cocoa powder, and baking soda, and stir until mixed.

3. Crack the eggs in another bowl, whisk in sweetener, egg, oil, butter, and vanilla until smooth, and then slowly whisk in flour mixture until incorporated.

4. Add zucchini and 1/3 cup chocolate chips and then fold until just mixed.

5. Take a mini loaf pan that fits into the air fryer, grease it with olive oil, then pour in the prepared batter and sprinkle remaining chocolate chips on top.

6. Open the fryer, place the loaf pan in it, close with its lid and cook for 30 minutes at 310 ºF until inserted toothpick into the bread slides out clean.

7. When air fryer beeps, open its lid, remove the loaf pan, then place it on a wire rack then let the bread cool in it for 20 minutes.

8. Take out the bread, let it cool completely, then cut it into slices and serve.

Per serving: Calories: 356Kcal; Fat: 17g; Protein: 5.1g; Carbohydrates: 49g; Sugar: 1g; Sodium: 214mg

CHAPTER 2: Sides and Vegetables

21. Sweet-and-Sour Mixed Veggies

Preparation time: 25 minutes

Cooking time: 10 minutes

Servings: 4

Ingredients:

- 1/2-pound sterling asparagus, cut into 1 1/2-inch piece
- 1/2-pound broccoli, cut into 1 1/2-inch piece
- 1/2-pound carrots, cut into 1 1/2-inch piece
- 2 tablespoons peanut oil
- Some salt and white pepper, to taste
- 1/2 cup water
- 4 tablespoons raisins
- 2 tablespoon honey
- 2 tablespoons apple cider vinegar

Directions:

1. Abode the vegetables in a single layer in the lightly greased cooking basket. Drizzle the peanut oil over the vegetables.
2. Sprinkle with salt and white pepper.
3. Cook at 380 °F for 15 minutes, shaking the basket halfway through the cooking time.
4. Add 1/2 cup of water to a saucepan; bring to a rapid boil and add the raisins, honey, and vinegar. Prepare for 5 to 7 minutes or 'til the sauce has reduced by half.
5. Spoon the sauce over the warm vegetables then serve immediately. Bon appétit!

Per serving: Calories: 153Kcal; Fat: 7.1g; Protein: 3.6g; Carbohydrates: 21.6g; Sugar: 14.2g; Sodium: 184mg

22. Carrot and Oat Balls

Preparation time: 25 minutes

Cooking time: 10 minutes

Servings: 3

Ingredients:

- 4 carrots, grated
- 1 cup rolled oats, ground
- 1 tablespoon butter, room temperature
- 1 tablespoon chia seeds
- 1/2 cup scallions, chopped
- 2 cloves garlic, minced
- 2 tablespoons tomato ketchup
- 1 teaspoon cayenne pepper
- 1/2 teaspoon sea salt
- 1/4 teaspoon ground black pepper
- 1/2 teaspoon ancho chili powder
- 1/4 cup fresh bread crumbs

Directions:

1. Start by preheating your Air Fryer to 380 °F.
2. In your bowl, mix all ingredients until everything is perfectly and smoothly mixed. Shape the butter into bite-sized balls.
3. Cook the balls for 15 minutes, shaking the basket halfway through the cooking time. Bon appétit!

Per serving: Calories: 215Kcal; Fat: 4.7g; Protein: 7.5g; Carbohydrates: 37.2g; Sugar: 5.6g; Sodium: 224mg

23. Fried Peppers with Sriracha Mayo

Preparation time: 20 minutes

Cooking time: 10 minutes

Servings: 2

Ingredients:

- 4 bell peppers, seeded and sliced (1-inch pieces
- 1 onion, sliced (1-inch pieces
- 1 tablespoon of olive oil
- 1/2 teaspoon of dried rosemary
- 1/2 teaspoon of dried basil
- Kosher salt, to taste
- 1/4 teaspoon of ground black pepper
- 1/3 cup of mayonnaise
- 1/3 teaspoon of Sriracha

Directions:

1. Toss the bell peppers and onions with olive oil, rosemary, basil, salt, and black pepper.
2. Place the peppers and onions on an even layer in the cooking basket. Cook at 400 °F for 12 to 14 minutes.
3. Meanwhile, make the sauce by whisking the mayonnaise and Sriracha. Serve immediately.

Per serving: Calories: 346Kcal; Fat: 34.1g; Protein: 2.3g; Carbohydrates: 9.5g; Sugar: 4.9g; Sodium: 214mg

24. Family Vegetable Gratin

Preparation time: 35 minutes

Cooking time: 10 minutes

Servings: 4

Ingredients:

- 1-lb. Chinese cabbage, roughly chopped
- 2 bell peppers, seeded and sliced
- 1 jalapeno pepper, seeded and sliced
- 1 onion, thickly sliced
- 2 garlic cloves, sliced
- ½ stick butter
- 1 cup. all-purpose flour
- 1 cup milk
- 1 cup cream cheese
- Sea salt and freshly ground black pepper, to taste
- ½ tsp. cayenne pepper
- 1 cup Monterey Jack cheese, shredded

Directions:

1. Heat a pan of salted water and bring to a boil. Boil the Chinese cabbage for 2 to 3 minutes. Transfer the Chinese cabbage to cold water to stop the cooking process.
2. Place the Chinese cabbage in a lightly greased casserole dish. Add the peppers, onion, and garlic.
3. Next, melt the butter in a saucepan over moderate heat. Gradually add the flour and cook for 2 minutes to form a paste.
4. Gradually pour in the milk, stirring continuously 'til a thick sauce form. Add the cream cheese.
5. Season with salt, black pepper, then cayenne pepper. Add the mixture to the casserole dish.
6. Top with the shredded Monterey Jack cheese and bake in the preheated Air Fryer at 390 °F for 25 minutes. Serve hot.

Per serving: Calories: 373Kcal; Fat: 26.1g; Protein: 18.7g; Carbohydrates: 17.7g; Sugar: 7.7g; Sodium: 194mg

25. Parmesan Broccoli and Asparagus

Preparation time: 20 minutes

Cooking time: 15 minutes

Servings: 4

Ingredients:

- ½ lb. asparagus, trimmed
- 1 broccoli head, florets separated
- Juice of 1 lime
- 1 tbsp. parmesan, grated
- 2 tbsp. olive oil
- Salt and black pepper to taste.

Directions:

1. Take a bowl and mix the asparagus with the broccoli and all other ingredients except the parmesan. Then, toss and transfer to your air fryer's basket and cook at 400°F for 15 minutes
2. Divide between plates, sprinkle the parmesan on top, and serve.

Per serving: Calories: 172Kcal; Fat: 5g; Protein: 9g; Carbohydrates: 4g; Sugar: 3.7g; Sodium: 164mg

26. Asparagus With Garlic

Preparation time: 5 minutes

Cooking time: 10 minutes

Servings: 4

Ingredients:

- 1-lb. asparagus, rinsed, ends snapped off where they naturally break (see Tip)
- tsp. olive oil
- 2 garlic cloves, minced
- 2 tbsp. balsamic vinegar
- ½ tsp. dried thyme

Directions:

1. In a huge bowl, mix the asparagus with olive oil. -Transfer to the air fryer basket.
2. Sprinkle with garlic. Roast for 4 to 5 minutes for crisp-tender or for 8 to 11 minutes for asparagus that is crisp on the outside and tender on the inside.
3. Drizzle with the balsamic vinegar and sprinkle with the thyme leaves. Serve immediately.

Per serving: Calories: 41Kcal; Fat: 1g; Protein: 3g; Carbohydrates: 6g; Sugar: 7.2g; Sodium: 234mg

27. Crunchy Cauliflower

Preparation time: 20 minutes

Cooking time: 15 minutes

Servings: 5

Ingredients:

- 2 oz. cauliflower
- 1 tbsp. potato starch
- 1 tsp. olive oil
- Salt & pepper to taste

Directions:

1. Set the air fryer toaster oven to 400°F and preheat it for 3 minutes. Slice cauliflower into equal pieces and if you are using potato starch then toss with the florets into the bowl.
2. Add some olive oil and mix to coat.
3. Use olive oil cooking spray for spraying the inside of the air fryer toaster oven basket then add cauliflower.
4. Cook for eight minutes then shake the basket and cook for another 5 minutes depending on your desired level of crispiness. Sprinkle roasted cauliflower with fresh parsley, kosher salt, and seasonings or sauce of your choice.

Per serving: Calories: 36Kcal; Fat: 1g; Protein: 1g; Carbohydrates: 5g; Sugar: 4.7g; Sodium: 188mg

28. Classic Fried Pickles

Preparation time: 20 minutes

Cooking time: 10 minutes

Servings: 2

Ingredients:

- 1 egg, whisked
- 2 tablespoons buttermilk
- 1/2 cup fresh breadcrumbs
- 1/4 cup Romano cheese, grated
- 1/2 teaspoon onion powder
- 1/2 teaspoon garlic powder
- 1 ½ cups dill pickle chips, pressed dry with kitchen towels
- Mayo Sauce:
- 1/4 cup mayonnaise
- 1/2 tablespoon mustard
- 1/2 teaspoon molasses
- 1 tablespoon ketchup
- 1/4 teaspoon ground black pepper

Directions:

1. In a narrow bowl, whisk the egg with buttermilk.
2. In another bowl, mix the breadcrumbs, cheese, onion powder, and garlic powder.
3. Dredge the pickle chips in the egg mixture, then, in the breadcrumb/cheese mixture.
4. Cook in your preheated Air Fryer at 400 °F for 5 minutes; shake the basket and cook for 5 minutes more.
5. Meanwhile, mix all the sauce ingredients until well combined. Serve the fried pickles with the mayo sauce for dipping.

Per serving: Calories: 342Kcal;Fat: 28.5g;Protein: 9.1g;Carbohydrates: 12.5g;Sugar: 4.9g; Sodium: 208mg

29. Spicy Glazed Carrots

Preparation time: 20 minutes

Cooking time: 10 minutes

Servings: 3

Ingredients:

- 1-pound carrots, cut into matchsticks
- 2 tablespoons peanut oil
- 1 tablespoon agave syrup
- 1 jalapeño, seeded and minced
- 1/4 teaspoon dill
- 1/2 teaspoon basil
- Salt and white pepper to taste

Directions:

1. Begin by warming your Air Fryer to 380 °F.
2. Toss all ingredients together and place them in the Air Fryer basket.
3. Prepare for 15 minutes, pulsating the basket halfway through the cooking time. Transfer to a serving platter and enjoy!

Per serving: Calories: 162Kcal; Fat: 9.3g; Protein: 1.4g;Carbohydrates: 20.1g; Sugar: 12.8g; Sodium: 170mg

30. Corn on the Cob with Herb Butter

Preparation time: 15 minutes

Cooking time: 10 minutes

Servings: 2

Ingredients:

- 2 ears new corn, shucked and cut into halves
- 2 tablespoons butter, room temperature
- 1 teaspoon granulated garlic
- 1/2 teaspoon fresh ginger, grated
- Sea salt and pepper, to taste
- 1 tablespoon fresh rosemary, chopped
- 1 tablespoon fresh basil, chopped

- 2 tablespoons fresh chives, roughly chopped

Directions:

1. Spritz the corn with cooking spray. Cook at 395 °F F for 6 minutes, turning them over halfway through the cooking time.

2. In the time being, mix the butter with the granulated garlic, ginger, salt, black pepper, rosemary, and basil.

3. Spread the butter mixture all over the corn on the cob. Cook in the preheated Air Fryer an additional 2 minutes. Bon appétit!

Per serving: Calories: 239Kcal; Fat: 13.3g; Protein: 5.4g; Carbohydrates: 30.2g; Sugar: 5.8g; Sodium: 258mg

31. Swiss Cheese & Vegetable Casserole

Preparation time: 50 minutes

Cooking time: 10 minutes

Servings: 4

Ingredients:

- 1-pound potatoes, peeled and sliced (1/4-inch thick
- 2 tablespoons olive oil
- 1/2 teaspoon red pepper flakes, crushed
- 1/2 teaspoon freshly ground black pepper
- Salt, to taste
- 3 bell peppers, thinly sliced
- 1 serrano pepper, thinly sliced
- 2 medium-sized tomatoes, sliced
- 1 leek, thinly sliced
- 2 garlic cloves, minced
- 1 cup Swiss cheese, shredded

Directions:

1. Begin by warming your Air Fryer to 350 °F. Spritz a casserole dish with cooking oil.

2. Place the potatoes in the casserole dish in an even layer; drizzle 1 tablespoon of olive oil over the top. Then place the red pepper, black pepper, and salt.

3. Add 2 bell peppers and 1/2 of the leeks. Add the tomatoes and the remaining 1 tablespoon of olive oil.

4. Add the remaining peppers, leeks, and minced garlic. Top with the cheese.

5. Cover the casserole with foil then bake for 32 minutes. Remove the foil and increase the temperature to 400 °F; bake an additional 16 minutes. Bon appétit!

Per serving: Calories: 328Kcal;Fat: 16.5g;Protein: 13.1g;Carbohydrates: 33.1g;Sugar: 7.6g; Sodium: 268mg

32. Three-Cheese Stuffed Mushrooms

Preparation time: 15 minutes

Cooking time: 10 minutes

Servings: 3

Ingredients:

- 9 large button mushrooms, stems removed
- 1 tablespoon olive oil
- Salt and ground black pepper, to taste
- 1/2 teaspoon dried rosemary
- 6 tablespoons Swiss cheese shredded
- 6 tablespoons Romano cheese, shredded
- 6 tablespoons cream cheese
- 1 teaspoon soy sauce
- 1 teaspoon garlic, minced
- 3 tablespoons green onion, minced

Directions:

1. Brush the mushroom caps with olive oil; sprinkle with salt, pepper, and rosemary.

2. In a mixing bowl, thoroughly combine the remaining ingredients, mix it well and divide the filling mixture among the mushroom caps.

3. Cook in your preheated Air Fryer at 390 °F for 7 minutes.

4. Let the mushrooms cool slightly before serving. Bon appétit!

Per serving: Calories: 345Kcal; Fat: 28g; Protein: 14.4g; Carbohydrates: 11.2g; Sugar: 3.6g; Sodium: 168mg

33. Sweet Corn Fritters with Avocado

Preparation time: 20 minutes

Cooking time: 10 minutes

Servings: 3

Ingredients:

- 2 cups sweet corn kernels
- 1 small-sized onion, chopped
- 1 garlic clove, minced
- 2 eggs, whisked
- 1 teaspoon baking powder
- 2 tablespoons fresh cilantro, chopped
- Sea salt & ground black pepper, to taste
- 1 avocado, peeled, pitted and diced
- 2 tablespoons sweet chili sauce

Directions:

1. In a mixing bowl, thoroughly combine the corn, onion, garlic, eggs, baking powder, cilantro, salt, and black pepper.

2. Shape the corn mixture into 6 patties and transfer them to the lightly greased Air Fryer basket.

3. Cook in the preheated Air Fry at 370°F for 8 minutes; turn them over and cook for 7 minutes longer.

4. Serve the cakes with the avocado and chili sauce to taste.

Per serving: Calories: 383Kcal; Fat: 21.3g; Protein: 12.7g; Carbohydrates: 42.8g; Sugar: 9.2g; Sodium: 188mg

34. Japanese Tempura Bowl

Preparation time: 20 minutes

Cooking time: 10 minutes

Servings: 3

Ingredients:

- 1 cup all-purpose flour
- Kosher salt& ground black pepper, to taste
- 1/2 teaspoon paprika
- 2 eggs
- 3 tablespoons soda water
- 1 cup panko crumbs
- 2 tablespoons olive oil
- 1 cup green beans
- 1 onion, cut into rings
- 1 zucchini, cut into slices
- 2 tablespoons soy sauce
- 1 tablespoon mirin
- 1 teaspoon dashi granules

Directions:

1. Mix the flour, salt, black pepper, and paprika in your shallow bowl. In a separate bowl, whisk the eggs and soda water. In a third shallow bowl, mix the panko crumbs with olive oil.

2. Dip the vegetables in flour mixture, then in the egg mixture; lastly, roll over the panko mixture to coat evenly.

3. Cook in your preheated Air Fryer at 400 °F for 10 minutes, shaking the basket halfway through the cooking time. Work

in batches until the vegetables are crispy and golden brown.

4. Then, make the sauce by whisking the soy sauce, mirin, and dashi granules. Bon appétit!

Per serving: Calories: 446Kcal;Fat: 14.7g;Protein: 14.6g;Carbohydrates: 63.5g;Sugar: 3.8g; Sodium: 238mg

35. Butter Endives

Preparation time: 15 minutes;

Cooking time: 15 minutes

Servings: 4

Ingredients:

- 4 endives, trimmed and halved
- Salt and black pepper to taste
- 1 tbsp. lime juice
- 1 tbsp. butter, melted

Directions:

1. Place the endives in your air fryer, then add the salt and pepper to taste, lemon juice, and butter.
2. Cook at a temperature of 360 o F for 10 minutes.
3. Cut into different plates and serve right away.

Per serving: Calories: 100Kcal; Fat: 3g;Protein: 4g; Carbohydrates: 8g; Sugar: 3.6g; Sodium: 218mg

36. Garlic-Roasted Bell Peppers

Preparation time: 5 minutes

Cooking time: 20 minutes

Servings: 4

Ingredients:

- 2 bell peppers, any colors, stemmed, seeded, membranes removed, and cut into fourths
- 1 tsp. olive oil
- 2 garlic cloves, minced

- ½ tsp. dried thyme

Directions:

1. Put the peppers in the basket of the air fryer and drizzle with olive oil. Then, toss it gently.
2. Roast for 15 minutes.
3. Sprinkle with garlic and thyme.
4. Roast for 3 to 5 minutes more, or until tender.
5. Serve immediately.

Per serving: Calories: 36Kcal; Fat: 1g; Protein: 1g; Carbohydrates: 5g; Sugar: 3.9g; Sodium: 298mg

37. Sweet Beets Salad

Preparation time: 20 minutes

Cooking time: 15 minutes

Servings: 4

Ingredients:

- 1 ½-lb. beets; peeled and quartered
- 2 tbsps. brown sugar
- 2 scallions; chopped
- 2 tbsp. cider vinegar
- ½ cup orange juice
- 2 cups Arugula
- 2 tbsps. mustard
- A drizzle olive oil
- 2 tbsps. orange zest; grated

Directions:

1. Season the beets with orange juice and oil in a bowl.
2. Spread the beets in the air fryer basket and seal the fryer.
3. Cook the beet for 10 minutes at 350°F on Air fryer mode.
4. Place these cooked beets in a bowl then toss in orange zest, arugula, and scallions.
5. Whisk mustard, vinegar, and sugar in a different bowl.

6. Add this mixture to the beets and mix well.

Per serving: Calories: 151Kcal; Fat: 2g; Protein: 4g; Carbohydrates: 14g; Sugar: 3g; Sodium: 188mg

38. Veg Buffalo Cauliflower

Preparation time: 20 minutes

Cooking time: 15 minutes

Servings: 3

Ingredients:

- 1 medium head cauliflower
- 1 tsp. avocado oil
- 2 tbsp. red hot sauce
- 1 tbsp. nutritional yeast
- 1 ½ tsp. maple syrup
- ¼ tsp. sea salt
- 1 tbsp. cornstarch or arrowroot starch

Directions:

1. Set your air fryer toaster oven to 360 °F. Place all the ingredients into your bowl except cauliflower. Mix them to combine.

2. Put the cauliflower and mix to coat equally. Put half of your cauliflower into an air fryer and cook for 15 minutes but keep shaking them until your get desired consistency.

3. Do the same for the remaining cauliflower and reduce the cooking time to 10 minutes.

4. Keep the cauliflower tightly sealed in the refrigerator for 3-4 days. When heating again, add back to the air fryer for 1-2 minutes until crispness.

Per serving: Calories: 248Kcal; Fat: 20g; Protein: 4g; Carbohydrates: 13g; Sugar: 4.8g; Sodium: 268mg

39. Baked Potato Topped With Cream Cheese and Olives

Preparation time:

Cooking time: 40 minutes

Servings: 1

Ingredients:

- 1/4 teaspoon onion powder
- 1 medium russet potato, scrubbed and peeled
- 1 tablespoon chives, chopped
- 1 tablespoon Kalamata olives
- 1 teaspoon olive oil
- 1/8 teaspoon salt
- a dollop of vegan butter
- a dollop of vegan cream cheese

Directions:

1. Place inside the air fryer basket and cook for 40 minutes. Be sure to turn the potatoes once halfway.

2. Place the potatoes in your mixing bowl and pour olive oil, onion powder, salt, and vegan butter.

3. Preheat the air fryer to 400 °FF.

4. Serve the potatoes with vegan cream cheese, Kalamata olives, chives, and other vegan toppings that you want.

Per serving: Calories: 145Kcal; Fat: 1g; Protein: 5g; Carbohydrates: 31g; Sugar: 2.8g; Sodium: 178mg

40. Spices Stuffed Eggplants

Preparation time: 10 minutes

Cooking time: 12 minutes

Servings: 4

Ingredients:

- 8 baby eggplants
- 4 teaspoons olive oil, divided
- 3/4 tablespoon dry mango powder

- 3/4 tablespoon ground coriander
- 1/2 teaspoon ground cumin
- 1/2 teaspoon ground turmeric
- 1/2 teaspoon garlic powder
- Salt, to taste

Directions:

1. Preheat the Air fryer to 370 °F and grease an Air fryer basket.
2. Make slits from the bottom of each eggplant leaving the stems intact.
3. Mix one teaspoon of oil and spices in a bowl and fill each slit of eggplants with this mixture.
4. Brush each eggplant's outer side with remaining oil and arrange in the Air fryer basket.
5. Cook for about 12 minutes and dish out in a serving plate to serve hot.

Per serving: Calories: 106Kcal; Fat: 3g; Protein: 3g; Carbohydrates: 20g; Sugar: 5g; Sodium: 249mg

CHAPTER 3: Beans and Grains

41. Spicy Seafood Risotto

Preparation time: 10 minutes

Cooking time: 25 minutes

Servings: 3

Ingredients:

- 1 ½ cups cooked rice, cold
- 3 tablespoons shallots, minced
- 2 garlic cloves, minced
- 1 tablespoon oyster sauce
- 2 tablespoons dry white wine
- 2 tablespoons sesame oil
- Salt and ground black pepper, to taste
- 2 eggs
- 4 ounces lump crab meat
- 1 teaspoon ancho chili powder
- 2 tablespoons fresh parsley, roughly chopped

Directions:

1. Mix the cold rice, shallots, garlic, oyster sauce, dry white wine, sesame oil, salt, and black pepper in a lightly greased baking pan. Stir in the whisked eggs.
2. Cook in your preheated air fryer at 370°F 13 to 16 minutes.
3. Add the crab and ancho chili powder to the baking dish; stir until everything is well combined. Cook for 6 more minutes.
4. Serve at room temperature, garnished with fresh parsley. Bon appétit!

Per serving: Calories: 445Kcal; Fat: 17g; Protein: 24g; Carbohydrates: 48g; Sugar: 5g; Sodium: 189mg

42. Mexican-Style Brown Rice Casserole

Preparation time: 15 minutes

Cooking time: 50 minutes

Servings: 4

Ingredients:

- 1 tablespoon olive oil
- 1 shallot, chopped
- 2 cloves garlic, minced
- 1 habanero pepper, minced
- 2 cups brown rice
- 3 cups chicken broth
- 1 cup water
- 2 ripe tomatoes, pureed
- Sea salt &ground black pepper, to taste
- 1/2 teaspoon dried Mexican oregano
- 1 teaspoon red pepper flakes
- 1 cup Mexican cotija cheese, crumbled

Directions:

1. In your nonstick skillet, heat the olive oil over a moderate flame. Once hot, cook the shallot, garlic, and habanero pepper until tender and fragrant; reserve.
2. Heat the brown rice, vegetable broth and water in a pot. Bring it to a boil then turn your stove down to simmer and cook for 35 minutes.
3. Grease a baking pan with nonstick cooking spray.
4. Spoon the cooked rice into the baking pan. Add the sautéed mixture. Spoon the tomato puree over the sautéed mixture. Sprinkle with salt, black pepper, oregano, and red pepper.

5. Cook in the preheated air fryer at 380°F for 8 minutes. Top with the cotija cheese and bake for 5 minutes longer or until cheese is melted. Enjoy!

Per serving: Calories 433Kcal; Fat 4g; Protein: 11g; Carbohydrates: 76g; Sugar: 8g; Sodium: 359mg

43. Japanese Chicken And Rice Salad

Preparation time: 15 minutes

Cooking time: 45 minutes

Servings: 4

Ingredients:

- 1-pound chicken tenderloins
- 2 tablespoons shallots, chopped
- 1 garlic clove, minced
- 1 red bell pepper, chopped
- 1 ½ cups brown rice
- 1 cup baby spinach
- 1/2 cup snow peas
- 2 tablespoons soy sauce
- 1 teaspoon yellow mustard
- 1 tablespoon rice vinegar
- 1 tablespoon liquid from pickled ginger
- 1 teaspoon agave syrup
- 2 tablespoons black sesame seeds, to serve
- 1/4 cup mandarin orange segments

Directions:

1. Start by preheating your air fryer to 380°F. Then, add the chicken tenderloins to the baking pan and cook until it starts to get crisp or about 6 minutes.
2. Add the shallots, garlic, and bell pepper. Cook for 6 more minutes. Wait for the chicken mixture to cool down completely and transfer to a salad bowl.
3. Bring 3 cups of water and 1 teaspoon of salt to a boil in a saucepan over medium-high heat. Stir in the rice then reduce the heat to simmer; cook about 20 minutes.
4. Let your rice sit in the covered saucepan for another 10 minutes. Drain the rice and allow it to cool completely.
5. Stir the cold rice into the salad bowl; add the baby spinach and snow peas. In a small mixing dish, whisk the soy sauce, mustard, rice vinegar, liquid from pickled ginger, and agave syrup.
6. Dress the salad and stir well to combine. Garnish with black sesame seeds and mandarin orange. Enjoy!

Per serving: Calories: 387Kcal; Fat: 7g; Protein24g; Carbohydrates: 69g; Sugar: 9g; Sodium: 339mg

44. Risotto Balls With Bacon And Corn

Preparation time: 15 minutes

Cooking time: 30 minutes

Servings: 6

Ingredients:

- 4 slices Canadian bacon
- 1 tablespoon olive oil
- 1/2 medium-sized leek, chopped
- 1 teaspoon fresh garlic, minced
- Sea salt & freshly ground pepper, to taste
- 1 cup white rice
- 4 cups vegetable broth
- 1/3 cup dry white wine
- 2 tablespoons tamari sauce
- 1 tablespoon oyster sauce
- 1 tablespoon butter
- 1 cup sweet corn kernels
- 1 bell pepper, seeded and chopped

- 2 eggs lightly beaten
- 1 cup breadcrumbs
- 1 cup parmesan cheese, preferably freshly grated

Directions:

1. Cook the Canadian bacon in a nonstick skillet over medium-high heat. Allow it to cool, finely chop, and reserve.
2. Heat the olive oil in your saucepan over medium heat. Now, sauté the leeks and garlic, occasionally stir for about 5 minutes. Add the salt and pepper.
3. Stir in the white rice. Continue to cook for approximately 3 minutes or until translucent. Add the warm broth, wine, tamari sauce, and oyster sauce; cook until the liquid is absorbed.
4. Remove your saucepan from the heat; stir in the butter, corn, bell pepper, and reserved Canadian bacon. Let it cool completely. Then, shape the mixture into small balls.
5. In a shallow bowl, combine the eggs with the breadcrumbs and parmesan cheese. Dip each ball in the eggs/crumb mixture.
6. Cook in the preheated air fryer at 395°F for 10 to 12 minutes, shaking the basket periodically. Serve warm.

Per serving: Calories: 435Kcal; Fat: 16g; Protein: 23g; Carbohydrates: 44g; Sugar: 1g; Sodium: 244mg

45. Cheese And Bacon Crescent Ring

Preparation time: 10 minutes
Cooking time: 25 minutes
Servings: 4
Ingredients:

- 1 (8-ounce) can crescent dough sheet

- 1 ½ cups Monterey jack cheese, shredded
- 4 slices bacon, cut chopped
- 4 tablespoons tomato sauce
- 1 teaspoon dried oregano

Directions:

1. Unroll the crescent dough sheet and separate into 8 triangles. Arrange the triangles on a piece of parchment paper; place the triangles in the ring so it should look like the sun.
2. Place the shredded Monterey jack cheese, bacon, and tomato sauce on the half of each triangle, at the center of the ring. Sprinkle with oregano.
3. Bring each triangle up over the filling. Press the overlapping dough to flatten. Transfer the parchment paper with the crescent ring to the air fryer basket.
4. Bake at 355°F for 20 minutes or until the ring is golden brown. Bon appétit!

Per serving: Calories: 506Kcal; Fat: 38g; Protein: 27g; Carbohydrates: 36g; Sugar: 9g; Sodium: 223mg

46. Paella-Style Spanish Rice

Preparation time: 10 minutes
Cooking time: 35 minutes
Servings: 2
Ingredients:

- 2 cups water
- 1 cup white rice, rinsed and drained
- 1 cube vegetable stock
- 1 chorizo, sliced
- 2 cups brown mushrooms, cleaned and sliced
- 2 cloves garlic, finely chopped
- 1/2 teaspoon fresh ginger, ground
- 1 long red chili, minced
- 1/4 cup dry white wine

- 1/2 cup tomato sauce
- 1 teaspoon smoked paprika
- Kosher salt & ground black pepper, to taste
- 1 cup green beans

Directions:

1. In your medium saucepan, bring the water to a boil. Add the rice and vegetable stock cube. Stir and reduce the heat. Cover and let it simmer for 20 minutes.
2. Then, place the chorizo, mushrooms, garlic, ginger, and red chili in the baking pan. Cook at 380°F for 6 minutes, stirring periodically.
3. Add the prepared rice to the casserole dish. Add the remaining ingredients and gently stir to combine.
4. Cook for 6 minutes, checking periodically to ensure even cooking. Serve in individual bowls and enjoy!

Per serving: Calories: 546Kcal; Fat: 14g; Protein: 16g; Carbohydrates: 97g; Sugar: 5g; Sodium: 456mg

47. Buckwheat And Potato Flat Bread

Preparation time: 10 minutes

Cooking time: 20 minutes

Servings: 4

Ingredients:

- 4 potatoes, medium-sized
- 1 cup buckwheat flour
- 1/2 teaspoon salt
- 1/2 teaspoon red chili powder
- 1/4 cup honey

Directions:

1. Put the potatoes into a huge saucepan; add water to cover by about 1 inch. Bring to a boil. Then, lower the heat and let your potatoes simmer about 8 minutes until they are fork tender.
2. Mash the potatoes and add the flour, salt, and chili powder. Create 4 balls and flatten them with a rolling pin
3. Bake in the preheated air fryer at 390 °F for 6 minutes. Serve warm with honey.

Per serving: Calories: 334Kcal; Fat: 2g; Protein: 4g; Carbohydrates: 73g; Sugar: 15g; Sodium: 490mg

48. Delicious Coconut Granola

Preparation time: 15 minutes

Cooking time: 40 minutes

Servings: 12

Ingredients:

- 2 cups rolled oats
- 2 tablespoons butter
- 1 cup honey
- 1/2 teaspoon coconut extract
- 1/2 teaspoon vanilla extract
- 1/4 cup sesame seeds
- 1/4 cup pumpkin seeds
- 1/2 cup coconut flakes

Directions:

1. Thoroughly combine all ingredients, except the coconut flakes; mix well.
2. Spread the mixture onto the air fryer trays. Spritz with nonstick cooking spray.
3. Bake at 230°F f for 25 minutes; rotate the trays, add the coconut flakes, then bake for a further 10 to 15 mins.
4. This granola can be stored in an airtight container for up to 3 weeks. Enjoy!

Per serving: Calories: 192Kcal; Fat: 1g; Protein: 3g; Carbohydrates: 32g; Sugar: 28g; Sodium: 259mg

49. Savory Cheesy Cornmeal Biscuits

Preparation time: 15 minutes
Cooking time: 35 minutes
Servings: 6
Ingredients:

- 2 cups all-purpose flour
- 1 teaspoon baking soda
- 1 teaspoon baking powder
- 1 teaspoon granulated sugar
- 1/4 teaspoon ground chipotle
- Sea salt, to taste
- A pinch of grated nutmeg
- 1 stick butter, cold
- 6 ounces canned whole corn kernels
- 1 cup Colby cheese, shredded
- 2 tablespoons sour cream
- 2 eggs, beaten

Directions:

1. In your mixing bowl, combine the flour, baking soda, baking powder, sugar, ground chipotle, salt, and a pinch of nutmeg.
2. Cut in the butter 'til the mixture resembles coarse crumbs. Stir in the corn, Colby cheese, sour cream, and eggs; stir until everything is well incorporated.
3. Turn the dough out onto a floured surface. Knead the dough with your hands and roll it out to 1-inch thickness. Using a 3-inch round cutter, cut out the biscuits.
4. Transfer the cornmeal biscuits to the lightly greased air fryer basket. Brush the biscuits with cooking oil.

5. Bake in the preheated air fryer at 400°F for 17 minutes. Continue cooking until all the batter is used. Bon appétit!

Per serving: Calories: 444Kcal; Fat: 27g; Protein: 14g; Carbohydrates: 36g; Sugar: 6g; Sodium: 249mg

50. Asian-Style Shrimp Pilaf

Preparation time: 15 minutes
Cooking time: 45 minutes
Servings: 3
Ingredients:

- 1 cup koshihikari rice, rinsed
- 1 yellow onion, chopped
- 2 garlic cloves, minced
- 1/2 teaspoon fresh ginger, grated
- 1 tablespoon shoyu sauce
- 2 tablespoons rice wine
- 1 tablespoon sushi seasoning
- 1 tablespoon caster sugar
- 1/2 teaspoon sea salt
- 5 ounces frozen shrimp, thawed
- 2 tablespoons katsuobushi flakes, for serving

Directions:

1. Place the koshihikari rice and 2 cups of water in a large saucepan then bring to a boil. Coverand then turn the heat down to low and continue cooking for 15 minutes more. Set aside for 10 minutes.
2. Mix the rice, onion, garlic, ginger, shoyu sauce, wine, sushi seasoning, sugar, and salt in a lightly greased baking dish.
3. Cook in your preheated air fryer at 370°F for 13 to 16 minutes.
4. Add the shrimp to the baking dish and gently stir until everything is well combined. Cook for 6 minutes more.

5. Serve at room temperature, garnished with katsuobushi flakes. Enjoy!

Per serving: Calories: 368Kcal; Fat: 3g; Protein: 9g; Carbohydrates: 64g; Sugar: 9g; Sodium: 199mg

51. Wild Rice Pilaf

Preparation time: 10 minutes
Cooking time: 25 minutes
Servings: 12
Ingredients:

- 1 shallot, chopped
- 1 tsp. garlic, minced
- A drizzle of olive oil
- 1 cup farro
- ¾ cup wild rice
- 4 cups chicken stock
- salt and black pepper to the taste
- 1 tbsp. parsley, chopped
- ½ cup hazelnuts, toasted and chopped
- ¾ cup cherries, dried
- chopped chives for serving

Directions:

1. In a dish that fits your air fryer, mix shallot with garlic, oil, faro, wild rice, stock, salt, pepper, parsley, hazelnuts, and cherries, stir, place in your air fryer's basket and cook at 350°F for 25 minutes.
2. Divide among plates and serve as a side dish.
3. Enjoy!

Per serving: Calories: 142Kcal; Fat: 4g; Protein: 4g; Carbohydrates: 22g; Sugar: 7g; Sodium: 209mg

52. Pumpkin Rice

Preparation time: 5 minutes
Cooking time: 30 minutes
Servings: 4
Ingredients:

- 2 tbsp. olive oil
- 1 small yellow onion, chopped
- 2 garlic cloves, minced
- 12 oz. white rice
- 4 cups chicken stock
- 6 oz. pumpkin puree
- ½ tsp. nutmeg
- 1 tsp. thyme, chopped
- ½ tsp. ginger, grated
- ½ tsp. Cinnamon powder
- ½ tsp. allspice
- 4 oz. heavy cream

Directions:

1. In a dish that fits your air fryer, mix oil with onion, garlic, rice, stock, pumpkin puree, nutmeg, thyme, ginger, cinnamon, allspice and cream, stir well, place in your air fryer's basket and cook at 360°F for 30 minutes.
2. Divide among plates and serve as a side dish.
3. Enjoy!

Per serving: Calories: 261Kcal; Fat: 6g; Protein: 4g; Carbohydrates: 18g; Sugar: 6g; Sodium: 187mg

53. Colored Veggie Rice

Preparation time: 10 minutes
Cooking time: 25 minutes
Servings: 4
Ingredients:

- 2 cups basmati rice
- 1 cup mixed carrots, peas, corn and green beans
- 2 cups water
- ½ tsp. green chili, minced

- ½ tsp. ginger, grated
- 3 garlic cloves, minced
- 2 tbsp. butter
- 1 tsp. cinnamon powder
- 1 tbsp. cumin seeds
- 2 bay leaves
- 3 whole cloves
- 5 black peppercorns
- 2 whole cardamoms
- 1 tbsp. sugar
- salt to the taste

Directions:

1. Put the water in a heatproof dish that fits your air fryer, add rice, mixed veggies, green chili, grated ginger, garlic cloves, cinnamon, cloves, butter, cumin seeds, bay leaves, cardamoms, black peppercorns, salt and sugar, stir, put in your air fryer's basket and cook at 370°F for 25 minutes.
2. Divide among plates and serve as a side dish.
3. Enjoy!

Per serving: Calories: 283Kcal;Fat: 4g;Protein: 14g;Carbohydrates: 28g; Sugar: 5g; Sodium: 264mg

54. Roasted Chickpeas

Preparation time: 35 minutes

Cooking time: 25 minutes

Servings: 6

Ingredients:

- 15-ounce cooked chickpeas
- 1 teaspoon garlic powder
- 1 tablespoon nutritional yeast
- 1/8 teaspoon cumin
- 1 teaspoon smoked paprika
- 1/2 teaspoon salt

- 1 tablespoon olive oil

Directions:

1. Take a large baking sheet, line it with paper towels, then spread chickpeas on it, cover the peas with paper towels, and let rest for 30 minutes or until chickpeas are dried.
2. Turn on the air fryer, place the fryer basket inside, coat it with olive oil, close the lid, set the temperature to 355°F, and preheat for five minutes.
3. Place dried chickpeas in a bowl, add remaining ingredients, and toss until well coated.
4. Open the fryer, add chickpeas in it, close with its lid and cook for 20 minutes until nicely golden and crispy, shaking the chickpeas every 5 minutes.
5. When air fryer beeps, open its lid, transfer chickpeas onto a serving bowl and serve.

Per serving: Calories: 124Kcal;Fat: 4.4g;Protein: 4.7g;Carbohydrates: 17.4g; Sugar: 7g; Sodium: 369mg

55. Air Fryer Risotto Balls

Preparation time: 20 minutes

Cooking time: 10 minutes

Servings: 4

Ingredients:

Risotto:

- 1 tbsp. olive oil
- 1 cup onions diced very small
- 4 cups vegetable broth
- 1 cup arborio rice
- 1 cup parmesan cheese

Breading:

- 1.5 cups Bread Crumbs
- 2 eggs beaten

Directions:

1. If using the leftover risotto, go to step 6.

2. Add some olive oil to a deep and large saucepan and heat it over medium heat. Post this, add the onions and sauté until soft.

3. Add dry rice to the pan and sauté for around 1 minute.

4. After this, add 2 cups of veggie broth. Let the broth cook down while continually stir to avoid any burning. Once the liquid has been cooked properly, add 2 more cups of veggie broth. Continue with this process until all the liquid is absorbed and your rice is soft. This process should take around 20 minutes. Stir in parmesan.

5. Put risotto into a casserole dish or sheet pan. Cool for around 1-2 hours in the fridge. (The risotto has to be properly cooled to be able to be rolled into balls).

6. Take a small bowl and place the bread crumbs in it. In another container, store the beaten eggs.

7. Remove the chilled risotto (rice mixture) from the fridge. Roll into 1-inch rice balls. Dip them into eggs then into bread crumbs to coat the entire ball. Do this until you run out of ingredients.

8. Place rolled and coated balls back into the fridge for 45 minutes.

9. Remove from the fridge and place it on the trays of the Instant Pot Duo Crisp Air Fryer in small batches. Choose the Air Fry option on the appliance and close the lid.

10. Air Fry at 400°F for a cooking time of 10 minutes. Shake for 8 minutes. The balls are properly done around minute 6-7 but the browning doesn't happen until minute 8-10.

11. Serve with marinara sauce.

Per serving: Calories: 255Kcal;Fat: 7g;Protein: 10g; Carbohydrates: 38g; Sugar: 0g; Sodium: 188mg

56. Fried Green Beans with Pecorino Romano

Preparation time: 15 minutes
Cooking time: 10 minutes
Servings: 3
Ingredients:

- 2 tbsp. of buttermilk.
- 1 egg.
- 4 tbsp. of cornmeal.
- 4 tbsp. of tortilla chips, crushed.
- 4 tbsp. of Pecorino Romano cheese, finely grated.
- Salt and crushed black pepper, to taste.
- 1 tsp. of smoked paprika.
- 12 oz. of green beans, trimmed.

Directions:

1. In your shallow bowl, whisk together the buttermilk and egg.

2. In a separate bowl, combine the cornmeal, tortilla chips, Pecorino Romano cheese, salt, black pepper, and paprika.

3. Dip the green beans in the egg mixture, then, in the cornmeal/cheese mixture. Place the green beans in the lightly greased cooking basket.

4. Cook in your preheated Air Fryer at 390°F for 4 mins. Shake the basket and then cook for a further 3 minutes.

5. Taste, adjust the seasonings and serve with the dipping sauce if desired. Bon appétit!

Per serving: Calories: 340Kcal;Fat: 9.7g;Protein: 12.8g;Carbohydrates: 50.9g;Sugar: 1g; Sodium: 191mg

57. Green Beans

Preparation time: 5 minutes

Cooking time: 13 minutes

Servings: 4

Ingredients:

- 1-pound of green beans.
- ¾ tsp. of garlic powder.
- ¾ tsp. of ground black pepper.
- 1 ¼ tsp. of salt.
- ½ tsp. of paprika.
- Olive oil.

Directions:

1. Switch on the Air Fryer, insert the fryer basket, grease it with olive oil, then shut with its lid, set the fryer to 400°F, and preheat for 5 minutes.
2. Meanwhile, place the beans in a bowl, spray generously with olive oil, sprinkle with garlic powder, black pepper, salt, and paprika and toss until well coated.
3. Open the fryer, add green beans to it, close with its lid, and cook for 8 minutes until nicely golden and crispy, shaking halfway through the frying.
4. When Air Fryer beeps, open its lid, transfer green beans onto a serving plate and serve.

Per serving: Calories: 45Kcal; Fat: 1g; Protein: 2g; Carbohydrates: 7g; Sugar: 0g; Sodium: 181mg

58. Saltine Wax Beans

Preparation time: 10 minutes

Cooking time: 7 minutes

Servings: 4

Ingredients:

- 1/2 cup flour
- 1 teaspoon smoky chipotle powder
- 1/2 teaspoon ground black pepper
- 1 teaspoon sea salt flakes
- 2 eggs, beaten
- 1/2 cup crushed saltines
- 10 ounces (283 g) wax beans
- Cooking spray

Directions:

1. Preheat the air fryer oven to 360F (182C).
2. Add the flour, chipotle powder, black pepper, and salt in a bowl. Put the eggs in second bowl. Put the crushed saltines in the third bowl.
3. Wash the beans with cold water and remove any stringy debris.
4. Before dipping the beans in the beaten egg, coat them with the flour mixture. Cover them with the saltine crumbs.
5. Spritz the beans with cooking spray, then transfer to the air fryer basket.
6. Move the baking pan to the fryer basket and set time to 4 minutes.
7. Give the air fryer basket a good shake and continue to air fry for 3 minutes. Serve hot.

Per serving: Calories: 35Kcal; Fat: 1g; Protein: 2g; Carbohydrates: 5g; Sugar: 3.7g; Sodium: 221mg

59. Easy Rosemary Green Beans

Preparation time: 5 minutes

Cooking time: 5 minutes

Servings: 1

Ingredients:

- 1 tablespoon butter, melted
- 2 tablespoons rosemary
- 1/2 teaspoon salt
- 3 cloves garlic, minced
- 3/4 cup chopped green beans

Directions:

1. Preheat the air fryer oven to 390F (199C).

2. Combine the melted butter with the rosemary, salt, and minced garlic.
3. Toss in the green beans, coating them well. Transfer to the air fryer basket. Set air fryer time to 5 minutes.
4. Serve immediately.

Per serving: Calories: 32Kcal; Fat: 0.3g;Protein: 2g; Carbohydrates: 8g; Sugar: 1.2; Sodium: 221mg

60. Lemony Green Beans

Preparation time: 10 minutes
Cooking time: 12 minutes
Servings: 3

Ingredients:

- 1-pound green beans, trimmed and halved
- 1 teaspoon butter, melted
- 1 tablespoon fresh lemon juice
- 1/4 teaspoon garlic powder

Directions:

1. Preheat the Air fryer to 400°F and grease an Air fryer basket.
2. Mix all the ingredients in a bowl and toss to coat well.
3. Arrange the green beans into the Air fryer basket and cook for about 12 minutes.
4. Dish out in a serving plate and serve hot.

Per serving: Calories: 60Kcal Fat: 3g; Protein: 2g; Carbohydrates: 7g; Sugar: 3.2g; Sodium: 295mg

CHAPTER 4: Fish and Seafood

61.Steamer Clams

Preparation time: 20 minutes

Cooking time: 7 minutes

Servings: 2

Ingredients:

- 25 littleneck clams, scrubbed
- 2 tablespoons water
- 2 tablespoons butter, melted
- 2 lemon wedges

Directions:

1. Place clams in a large bowl filled with water. Allow it to rise for 10 minutes. Drain. Refill bowl with water and allow it to rise for another 10 minutes. Then, drain it.
2. Preheat air fryer at 350°F for 3 minutes.
3. Pour 2 tablespoons water into bottom of air fryer. Add clams to ungreased air fryer basket. Cook 7 minutes. Discard any clams that don't open.
4. Remove clams from shells and add to a large serving dish with melted butter. Squeeze lemon on top and serve.

Per serving: Calories: 279Kcal; Fat: 14g; Protein: 30g; Carbohydrates: 7g; Sugar: 0g; Sodium: 429mg

62. Bay Scallops

Preparation time: 5 minutes

Cooking time: 5 minutes

Servings: 4

Ingredients:

- 2 tablespoons butter, melted
- Juice from 1 medium lime
- ¼ teaspoon salt
- 1-pound bay scallops

Directions:

1. Preheat air fryer at 350°Ffor 3 minutes.
2. Whisk together butter, lime juice, and salt in a medium bowl. Add scallops and mix well.
3. Place scallops in ungreased air fryer basket. Cook 2 minutes. Toss scallops. Cook an additional 3 minutes.
4. Transfer scallops to a serving dish. Serve warm.

Per serving: Calories: 132Kcal; Fat: 6g; Protein: 14g; Carbohydrates: 4g; Sugar: 0g; Sodium: 591mg

63. Smoky Fried Calamari

Preparation time: 15 minutes

Cooking time: 8 minutes

Servings: 4

Ingredients:

- 2 tablespoons no-sugar-added tomato paste
- 1 tablespoon gochujang
- 1 tablespoon fresh lime juice
- 1 teaspoon smoked paprika
- ½ teaspoon salt
- 1 cup crushed pork rinds
- ⅓ pound (about 6) calamari tubes, cut into ¼" rings

Directions:

1. Preheat air fryer at 400°F for 3 minutes.
2. In your medium-sized bowl, whisk tomato paste, gochujang, lime juice, paprika, and salt together. Add pork rinds to a separate shallow dish.

3. Dredge a calamari ring in tomato mixture. Shake off excess. Roll through pork rind crumbs. Repeat with remaining rings.

4. Place half of calamari rings in air fryer basket lightly greased with olive oil. Cook 2 minutes. Gently flip then cook an additional 2 minutes.

5. Transfer cooked calamari to a large serving dish and repeat cooking with remaining calamari. Serve warm.

Per serving: Calories: 99Kcal; Fat: 3g; Protein: 11g; Carbohydrates: 6g; Sugar: 2g; Sodium: 545mg

64. Breaded Fish Sticks with Tartar Sauce

Preparation time: 10 minutes

Cooking time: 20 minutes

Servings: 4

Ingredients:

For Tartar Sauce:

- ½ cup mayonnaise
- 1 tablespoon Dijon mustard
- ½ cup small-diced dill pickles
- ⅛ teaspoon salt
- ¼ teaspoon freshly ground black pepper

For Fish Sticks:

- 1 large egg, beaten
- ¼ cup arrowroot flour
- ¼ cup almond flour
- ½ teaspoon salt
- ¼ teaspoon freshly ground black pepper
- 1-pound cod, cut into 1" sticks

Directions:

1. To make Tartar Sauce: Combine all ingredients in a small bowl and refrigerate covered until ready to use.

2. To make Fish Sticks: Preheat air fryer at 350°F for 3 minutes.

3. Place egg in a small bowl. Combine arrowroot flour, almond flour, salt, and pepper in a separate shallow dish.

4. Dip a fish stick in egg. Shake off excess egg. Roll in flour mixture. Transfer to a large plate. Repeat with remaining fish sticks.

5. Place half of fish sticks in air fryer basket lightly greased with olive oil. Cook 5 minutes. Carefully flip fish sticks. Cook an additional 5 minutes.

6. Transfer cooked fish sticks to a large serving plate and repeat cooking with remaining fish sticks. Serve warm with tartar sauce on the side.

Per serving: Calories: 363Kcal; Fat: 26g; Protein: 21g; Carbohydrates: 9g; Sugar: 1g; Sodium: 855mg

65. Tuna Melts On Tomatoes

Preparation time: 10 minutes

Cooking time: 4 minutes

Servings: 2

Ingredients:

- 1 (6-ounce) can tuna in water, drained
- ¼ cup mayonnaise
- 2 teaspoons yellow mustard
- 1 tablespoon minced dill pickle
- 1 tablespoon minced celery
- 1 tablespoon peeled and minced yellow onion
- ⅛ teaspoon salt
- ⅛ teaspoon freshly ground black pepper

- 4 thick slices large beefsteak tomato
- 1 small avocado, peeled, pitted, & cut into 8 slices
- ½ cup grated mild Cheddar cheese

Directions:

1. Combine tuna, mayonnaise, mustard, pickles, celery, onion, salt, and pepper in a medium bowl.
2. Preheat air fryer at 350°F for 3 minutes.
3. Cut a piece of parchment paper to fit the bottom of the air fryer basket. Place tomato slices on paper in single layer. Place two avocado slices on each tomato slice. Distribute tuna salad over avocado slices. Top evenly with cheese.
4. Place stacks in ungreased air fryer basket and cook 4 minutes until cheese starts to brown. Serve warm.

Per serving: Calories: 532Kcal; Fat: 46g; Protein: 22g; Carbohydrates: 13g; Sugar: 3g; Sodium: 762mg

66. Fish Taco

Preparation time: 10 minutes

Cooking time: 13 minutes

Servings: 4

Ingredients:

- 12 oz. cod filet
- 1 cup friendly bread crumbs
- 4 – 6 friendly flour tortillas
- 1 cup tempura butter
- ½ cup salsa
- ½ cup guacamole
- 2 tbsp. freshly chopped cilantro
- ½ tsp. salt
- ¼ tsp. black pepper
- Lemon wedges for garnish

Directions:

1. Slice the cod filets lengthwise and sprinkle salt and pepper on all sides.
2. Put the tempura butter in a bowl and coat each cod piece in it. Dip the fillets into the bread crumbs.
3. Pre-heat the Air Fryer to 340°F.
4. Fry the cod sticks for about 10 – 13 minutes in the fryer. Flip each one once while cooking.
5. In the meantime, coat one side of each tortilla with an even spreading of guacamole.
6. Put a cod stick in each tortilla and add the chopped cilantro and salsa on top. Lightly drizzle over the lemon juice. Fold into tacos.

Per serving: Calories: 705Kcal; Fat: 55.2g; Protein: 20.71g; Carbohydrates: 34.02g; Sugar: 5g; Sodium: 532mg

67. Seafood Fritters

Preparation time: 20 minutes

Cooking time: 30 minutes

Servings: 2-4

Ingredients:

- 2 cups clam meat
- 1 cup shredded carrot
- ½ cup shredded zucchini
- 1 cup flour, combined with 3/4 cup water to make a batter
- 2 tbsp. olive oil
- ¼ tsp. pepper

Directions:

1. Pre-heat your Air Fryer to 390 deg. F.
2. Add the clam meat with the olive oil, shredded carrot, pepper and zucchini together.

3. Using your hands, shape equal portions of the mixture into balls and roll each ball in the chickpea mixture.
4. Put the balls in the fryer and cook for 30 minutes, ensuring they turn nice and crispy before serving.

Per serving: Calories: 265Kcal; Fat: 8.89g; Protein: 5.9g; Carbohydrates: 40.02g; Sugar: 0g; Sodium: 458mg

68. Classic Lobster Salad

Preparation time: 10 minutes
Cooking time: 8 minutes
Servings: 2
Ingredients:

- 2 (6-ounce) uncooked lobster tails, thawed
- ¼ cup mayonnaise
- 2 teaspoons fresh lemon juice
- 1 small stalk celery, sliced
- 2 teaspoons chopped fresh chives
- 2 teaspoons chopped fresh tarragon
- ¼ teaspoon salt
- ⅛ teaspoon freshly ground black pepper
- 2 thick slices large beefsteak tomato
- 1 small avocado, peeled, pitted, and diced

Directions:

1. Preheat air fryer at 400°F for 3 minutes.
2. Using kitchen shears, cut down the middle of each lobster tail on the softer side. Carefully run your finger between the lobster meat and the shell to loosen meat.
3. Place lobster tails, cut sides up, in ungreased air fryer basket. Cook 8 minutes.
4. Transfer tails to a large plate and let cool about 3 minutes until easy to handle, then pull lobster meat from shell. Roughly chop meat and add to a medium bowl.

5. Add mayonnaise, lemon juice, celery, chives, tarragon, salt, and pepper to bowl. Combine.
6. Divide lobster salad between two medium plates, top with tomato slices, and garnish with avocado. Serve.

Per serving: Calories: 463Kcal; Fat: 36g; Protein: 24g; Carbohydrates: 12g; Sugar: 3g; Sodium: 1,343mg

69. Baked Avocados with Smoked Salmon

Preparation time: 10 minutes
Cooking time: 8 minutes
Servings: 2
Ingredients:

- ¼ cup apple cider vinegar
- 1 teaspoon granular erythritol
- ¼ cup peeled and sliced red onion
- 2 ounces cream cheese, room temperature
- 1 tablespoon capers, drained
- 2 large avocados, peeled, halved, and pitted
- 4 ounces smoked salmon
- 2 medium cherry tomatoes, halved

Directions:

1. In a mini saucepan, heat apple cider vinegar and erythritol over high heat 4 minutes until boiling. Add onion and remove saucepan from heat. Let set while preparing remaining ingredients. Drain when ready to use onions.
2. Combine cream cheese and capers in a small bowl. Cover and refrigerate until ready to use.
3. Preheat air fryer at 350°F for 3 minutes.
4. Place avocado halves, cut sides up, in ungreased air fryer basket and cook 4 minutes.

5. Transfer avocados to two medium plates and garnish with cream cheese mixture, smoked salmon, pickled onions, and tomato halves. Serve.

Per serving: Calories: 501Kcal; Fat: 42g; Protein: 16g; Carbohydrates: 22g; Sugar: 3g; Sodium: 590mg

70. Breaded Cod Sticks

Preparation time: 10 minutes
Cooking time: 12 minutes
Servings: 5
Ingredients:

- 2 Large eggs
- 3 tbsp. Milk
- 2 cups Breadcrumbs
- 1 cup Almond flour
- 1 lb. Cod

Directions:

1. Heat the Air Fryer at 350º Fahrenheit.
2. Prepare three bowls; one with the milk and eggs, one with the breadcrumbs (salt and pepper if desired), and another with almond flour.
3. Dip the sticks in the flour, egg mixture, and breadcrumbs.
4. Place in the basket and set the timer for 12 minutes. Toss the basket halfway through the cooking process.
5. Serve with your favorite sauce.

Per serving: Calories: 107Kcal; Fat: 3.69g; Protein: 16.56g; Carbohydrates: 0.74g; Sugar: 6g; Sodium: 562mg

71. Avocado Shrimp

Preparation time: 10 minutes
Cooking time: 10 minutes
Servings: 2

Ingredients:

- ½ cup onion, chopped
- 2 lb. shrimp
- 1 tbsp. seasoned salt
- 1 avocado
- ½ cup pecans, chopped

Directions:

1. Pre-heat the fryer at 400°F.
2. Put the chopped onion in the basket of the fryer and spritz with some cooking spray. Leave to cook for five minutes.
3. Add the shrimp and set the timer for a further five minutes. Sprinkle with some seasoned salt, then allow to cook for an additional five minutes.
4. During these last five minutes, halve your avocado and remove the pit. Cube each half, then scoop out the flesh.
5. Take care when removing the shrimp from the fryer. Place it on a dish and top with the avocado and the chopped pecans.

Per serving: Calories: 770Kcal; Fat: 37.92g; Protein: 98.97g; Carbohydrates: 14.69g; Sugar: 5g; Sodium: 772mg

72. Cheesy Lemon Halibut

Preparation time: 10 minutes
Cooking time: 12 minutes
Servings: 2
Ingredients:

- 1 lb. halibut fillet
- ½ cup butter
- 2 ½ tbsp. mayonnaise
- 2 ½ tbsp. lemon juice
- ¾ cup parmesan cheese, grated

Directions:

1. Pre-heat your fryer at 375°F.

2. Spritz the halibut fillets with cooking spray and season as desired.

3. Put the halibut in the fryer and cook for twelve minutes.

4. In the meantime, combine the butter, mayonnaise, and lemon juice in a bowl with a hand mixer. Ensure a creamy texture is achieved.

5. Stir in the grated parmesan.

6. When the halibut is ready, open the drawer and spread the butter over the fish with a butter knife. Allow to cook for a further two mins., then serve hot.

Per serving: Calories: 1328Kcal; Fat: 106.33g; Protein: 67.69g; Carbohydrates: 27.55g; Sugar: 5g; Sodium: 552mg

73. Crab Cakes With Arugula And Blackberry Salad

Preparation time: 15 minutes

Cooking time: 10 minutes

Servings: 2

Ingredients:

For Crab Cakes

- 8 ounces lump crabmeat, shells discarded
- 2 tablespoons mayonnaise
- ½ teaspoon Dijon mustard
- ½ teaspoon lemon juice
- 2 teaspoons peeled and minced yellow onion
- ¼ teaspoon prepared horseradish
- ¼ cup almond meal
- 1 large egg white, beaten
- ½ teaspoon Old Bay Seasoning

For Salad

- 1 tablespoon olive oil
- 2 teaspoons lemon juice
- ⅛ teaspoon salt
- ⅛ teaspoon freshly ground black pepper
- 4 ounces fresh arugula
- ½ cup fresh blackberries
- ¼ cup walnut pieces
- 2 lemon wedges

Directions:

1. To make Crab Cakes: Preheat air fryer at 400°F for 3 minutes.

2. In your medium bowl, combine all ingredients. Form into four patties.

3. Place patties into air fryer basket lightly greased with olive oil. Cook 5 minutes. Flip patties. Cook an additional 5 minutes.

4. Transfer crab cakes to a large plate. Set aside.

5. To make Salad: In a large bowl, whisk together olive oil, lemon juice, salt, and pepper. Add arugula and toss. Distribute into two medium bowls.

6. Add two crab cakes to each bowl. Garnish with blackberries, walnuts, and lemon wedges. Serve.

Per serving: Calories: 406Kcal; Fat: 29g; Protein: 29g; Carbohydrates: 10g; Sugar: 4g; Sodium: 790mg

74. Bacon-Wrapped Stuffed Shrimp

Preparation time: 10 minutes

Cooking time: 18 minutes

Servings: 4

Ingredients:

- 1-pound (about 20) large raw shrimp, deveined and shelled
- 3 tablespoons crumbled goat cheese
- 2 tablespoons panko bread crumbs
- ¼ teaspoon Worcestershire sauce
- ½ teaspoon prepared horseradish

- ¼ teaspoon garlic powder
- 2 teaspoons mayonnaise
- ¼ teaspoon freshly ground black pepper
- 2 tablespoons water
- 5 slices bacon, quartered
- ¼ cup chopped fresh parsley

Directions:

1. Butterfly shrimp by cutting down the spine of each shrimp without going all the way through.

2. In your medium bowl, combine goat cheese, bread crumbs, Worcestershire sauce, horseradish, garlic powder, mayonnaise, and pepper.

3. Preheat air fryer at 400°F for 3 minutes. Pour 2 tablespoons water into bottom of air fryer.

4. Evenly press goat cheese mixture into shrimp. Wrap a piece of bacon around each piece of shrimp to hold in cheese mixture.

5. Place half of shrimp in fryer basket. Cook 5 minutes. Flip shrimp. Cook an additional 4 minutes. Transfer to serving plate. Repeat with remaining shrimp.

6. Garnish with chopped parsley. Serve warm.

Per serving: Calories: 174Kcal; Fat: 8g; Protein: 20g; Carbohydrates: 4g; Sugar: 0g; Sodium: 833mg

75. Simply Shrimp

Preparation time: 5 minutes

Cooking time: 6 minutes

Servings: 2

Ingredients:

- 1-pound medium raw shrimp, tail on, deveined, and thawed or fresh
- 2 tablespoons butter, melted

- 1 tablespoon fresh lemon juice (about ½ medium lemon)

Directions:

1. Preheat air fryer at 350°F for 3 minutes.

2. In a large bowl, toss shrimp in butter.

3. Place shrimp in air fryer basket lightly greased with olive oil. Cook 4 minutes. Gently flip shrimp. Cook an additional 2 minutes.

4. Transfer shrimp to a large serving plate. Squeeze lemon juice over shrimp and serve.

Per serving: Calories: 265Kcal; Fat: 14g; Protein: 31g; Carbohydrates: 3g; Sugar: 0g; Sodium: 1,285mg

76. Chili Lime–Crusted Halibut

Preparation time: 10 minutes

Cooking time: 10 minutes

Servings: 2

Ingredients:

- 2 tablespoons butter, melted
- ½ cup crushed chili lime–flavored pork rinds
- 2 (6-ounce) halibut fillets

Directions:

1. Preheat air fryer at 350°F for 3 minutes.

2. Combine butter and pork rinds in a small bowl. Press mixture onto tops of halibut fillets.

3. Place fish in air fryer basket lightly greased with olive oil. Cook 10 minutes until fish is opaque and flakes easily with a fork.

4. Transfer fish to two medium plates and serve warm.

Per serving: Calories: 269Kcal; Fat: 15g; Protein: 32g; Carbohydrates: 0g; Sugar: 0g; Sodium: 239mg

77. Tuna Croquettes

Preparation time: 15 minutes

Cooking time: 24 minutes

Servings: 4

Ingredients:

- 1 (12-ounce) can tuna in water, drained
- ⅓ cup mayonnaise
- 1 tablespoon minced fresh celery
- 2 teaspoons dried dill, divided
- 1 teaspoon fresh lime juice
- 1 cup crushed pork rinds, divided
- 1 large egg
- 1 teaspoon prepared horseradish

Directions:

1. Preheat air fryer at 375°F for 3 minutes.
2. In a medium bowl, combine tuna, mayonnaise, celery, 1 teaspoon dill, lime juice, ¼ cup pork rinds, egg, and horseradish.
3. Form mixture into twelve rectangular mound shapes (about 2 tablespoons each). Roll each croquette in a shallow dish with remaining crushed pork rinds.
4. Place six croquettes in air fryer basket lightly greased with olive oil. Cook 4 minutes. Gently turn one third. Cook an additional 4 minutes. Gently turn another third. Cook an additional 4 minutes.
5. Transfer cooked croquettes to a large serving dish. Repeat cooking with remaining croquettes and garnish with remaining dill. Serve warm.

Per serving: Calories: 241Kcal; Fat: 18g; Protein: 19g; Carbohydrates: 0g; Sugar: 0g; Sodium: 440mg

78. Thyme Scallops

Preparation time: 5 minutes

Cooking time: 7 minutes

Servings: 1

Ingredients:

- 1 lb. scallops
- Salt and pepper
- ½ tbsp. butter
- ½ cup thyme, chopped

Directions:

1. Wash the scallops and dry them completely. Season with pepper and salt, then set aside while you prepare the pan.
2. Grease a foil pan in several spots with the butter and cover the bottom with the thyme. Place the scallops on top.
3. Pre-heat the fryer at 400°F and set the rack inside.
4. Place the foil pan on the rack and allow to cook for seven minutes.
5. Take care when removing the pan from the fryer and transfer the scallops to a serving dish. Spoon any remaining butter in the pan over the fish and enjoy.

Per serving: Calories: 484Kcal; Fat: 14.51g; Protein: 62.9g; Carbohydrates: 23.58g; Sugar: 2g; Sodium: 1162mg

79. Shrimp Spring Rolls with Sweet Chili Sauce

Preparation time: 20 minutes

Cooking time: 20 minutes

Servings: 4

Ingredients:

- 2 ½ tbsp. sesame oil, divided
- 1 cup julienne-cut red bell pepper
- 1 cup matchstick carrots
- 2 cups pre-shredded cabbage

- ¼ cup chopped fresh cilantro
- 2 tsp fish sauce
- ¼ tsp crushed red pepper
- 1 tbsp. fresh lime juice
- 3/4 cup julienne-cut snow peas
- 4 oz. peeled, deveined raw shrimp, chopped
- 8 (8-inch-square) spring roll wrappers
- ½ cup sweet chili sauce

Directions:

1. Get a large skillet, pour in 1.5 teaspoons of the oil and let it heat over high heat until it smokes slightly. Now toss in the bell pepper, carrots, and cabbage. Allow it to cook while continually stirring until the mixture is lightly wilted (this takes 1 or 1.5 minutes). Spread on a rimmed baking sheet then allow to cool for 5 minutes.

2. Get a large bowl and combine cilantro, fish sauce, crushed red pepper, lime juice, snow peas, shrimps, and the cabbage mixture. Stir slightly.

3. Place the spring roll wrappers on the work surface such that one corner is facing you. Using your spoon, transfer ¼ cup filling into the center of each spring roll wrapper, while spreading it from left to right and into a 3-inch long strip.

4. Fold the bottom corner of each wrapper over the filling, while tucking the tip of the corner under the filling. Fold right and left corners over filling. Brush the re-maining corner lightly using water, and roll the filled end of the wrapper towards the remaining corner. Finally, press gently to seal. Brush the spring rolls with the un-used two teaspoons oil.

5. Transfer the first four spring rolls in the air fryer basket and allow them to cook for about 7 minutes at 390°F. After the first

five minutes, turn the spring rolls. Do the same for the other spring rolls.

6. Serve the cooked spring rolls alongside sweet chili sauce.

Per serving: Calories: 1712Kcal; Fat: 21.1g; Protein: 61.22g; Carbohydrates: 310.7g; Sugar: 6g; Sodium: 672mg

80. Gambas with Sweet Potato

Preparation time: 10 minutes

Cooking time: 25 minutes

Servings: 3-4

Ingredients:

- 12 King prawns
- 4 garlic cloves
- 1 red chili pepper, de-seeded
- 1 shallot
- 4 tbsp. olive oil
- Smoked paprika powder
- 5 large sweet potatoes
- 2 tbsp. olive oil
- 1 tbsp. honey
- 2 tbsp. fresh rosemary, finely chopped
- 4 stalks lemongrass
- 2 limes

Directions:

1. Clean and gut the prawns.

2. Gut the garlic and red chili pepper finely, and chop the shallots.

3. Combine the red chili pepper, garlic, and olive oil alongside the paprika to form a marinade. Let the prawns marinate for about 2 hours in the marinade.

4. Make fine slices by cutting the sweet potato. Mix the potato slices with 2 table-spoons of olive oil, honey, and the chopped rosemary. Bake the potatoes in the air fryer at 360°F for 15 minutes.

5. While baking the potatoes, thread the prawns on the lemongrass stalks. Increase the temperature to 390°F and include the prawn skewers.

6. Allow the combination to cook for 5 minutes.

7. Serve alongside lime wedges.

Per serving: Calories: 465Kcal; Fat: 22.6g; Protein: 10.07g; Carbohydrates: 60.98g; Sugar: 4g; Sodium: 452mg

CHAPTER 5: Meat Recipes: Beef, Pork, Lamb, Poultry

81. Italian Beef Meatballs

Preparation time: 10 minutes

Cooking time: 15 minutes

Servings: 6

Ingredients:

- 2 large eggs
- 2 pounds ground beef
- ¼ cup fresh parsley, chopped
- 1¼ cups panko breadcrumbs
- ¼ cup Parmigiano Reggiano, grated
- 1 teaspoon dried oregano
- 1 small garlic clove, chopped
- Salt and black pepper, to taste
- 1 teaspoon vegetable oil

Directions:

1. Preheat Air fryer to 350°F and grease an Air fryer basket.
2. Mix beef with all other ingredients in a bowl until well combined.
3. Make equal-sized balls from the mixture and arrange the balls in the Air fryer basket.
4. Cook for about 13 minutes and dish out to serve warm.

Per serving: Calories: 398Kcal; Fat: 13.8g; Protein: 51.8g; Carbohydrates: 3.6g; Sugar: 1.3g; Sodium: 272mg

82. Beef and Veggie Spring Rolls

Preparation time: 10 minutes

Cooking time: 14 minutes

Servings: 8

Ingredients:

- 2-ounce Asian rice noodles, soaked in warm water, drained and cut into small lengths
- 7-ounce ground beef
- 1 small onion, chopped
- 1 cup fresh mixed vegetables
- 1 packet spring roll skins
- 2 tablespoons olive oil
- Salt and black pepper, to taste

Directions:

1. Preheat Air fryer to 350°F and oil the Air fryer basket.
2. Heat olive oil in a pan and add the onion and garlic.
3. Sauté for about 5 minutes and stir in the beef.
4. Cook for about 5 minutes and add vegetables and soy sauce.
5. Cook for about 7 minutes and stir in the noodles.
6. Place the spring rolls skin onto a smooth surface and put the filling mixture diagonally in it.
7. Fold in both sides to seal properly and brush with oil.
8. Arrange the rolls in batches in the Air fryer basket and cook for about 14 minutes, tossing in between.
9. Cook for about 15 minutes, flipping once in between and dish out in a platter.

Per serving: Calories: 147Kcal; Fat: 5.4g; Protein: 8.7g; Carbohydrates: 15.9g; Sugar: 0.6g; Sodium: 302mg

83. Beef Pot Pie

Preparation time: 10 minutes

Cooking time: 1 hour 27 minutes

Servings: 3

Ingredients:

- 1 pound beef stewing steak, cubed
- 1 can ale mixed into 1 cup water
- 2 beef bouillon cubes
- 1 tablespoon plain flour
- 1 prepared short crust pastry
- 1 tablespoon olive oil
- 1 tablespoon tomato puree
- 2 tablespoons onion paste
- Salt and black pepper, to taste

Directions:

1. Preheat the Air fryer to 390°F and grease 2 ramekins lightly.
2. Heat olive oil in a pan and add steak cubes.
3. Cook for about 5 minutes then stir in the onion paste and tomato puree.
4. Cook for about 6 minutes and add the ale mixture, bouillon cubes, salt and black pepper.
5. Bring to a boil and reduce the heat to simmer for about 1 hour.
6. Mix flour and 3 tablespoons of warm water in a bowl and slowly add this mixture into the beef mixture.
7. Roll out the short crust pastry and line 2 ramekins with pastry.
8. Divide the beef mixture evenly in the ramekins and top with extra pastry.
9. Transfer into the Air fryer and cook for about 10 minutes.
10. Set the Air fryer to 335°F and cook for about 6 more minutes.
11. Dish out and serve warm.

Per serving: Calories: 442Kcal; Fat: 14.2g; Protein: 50.6g; Carbohydrates: 19g; Sugar: 1.2g; Sodium: 583mg

84. Sage Beef

Preparation time: 10 minutes

Cooking time: 30 minutes

Servings: 4

Ingredients:

- 2pounds beef stew meat, cubed
- 1tablespoon sage, chopped
- 2tablespoons butter, melted
- ½ teaspoon coriander, ground
- ½ tablespoon garlic powder
- 1teaspoon Italian seasoning
- Salt and black pepper to the taste

Directions:

1. In the air fryer's pan, mix the beef with the sage, melted butter and the other ingredients, introduce the pan in the fryer and cook at 360°F for 30 minutes.
2. Divide everything between plates and serve.

Per serving: Calories: 290Kcal; Fat: 11g; Protein: 29g; Carbohydrates: 20g; Sugar: 3g; Sodium: 662mg

85. Pork Tenderloin with Bell Peppers

Preparation time: 20 minutes

Cooking time: 15 minutes

Servings: 3

Ingredients:

- 1 large green bell pepper, cutted in strips
- 1 red onion, thinly sliced
- 2 teaspoons Herbs de Provence
- Salt and ground black pepper, as required
- 1 tablespoon olive oil

- 10½-ounces pork tenderloin, cut into 4 pieces
- ½ tablespoon Dijon mustard

Directions:

1. In a bowl, add the bell pepper, onion, Herbs de Provence, salt, black pepper, and ½ tablespoon of oil and toss to coat well.
2. Rub the pork pieces with mustard, salt, and black pepper.
3. Drizzle with the remaining oil.
4. Set the temperature of air fryer to 390°F. Grease an air fryer pan.
5. Place bell pepper mixture into the prepared Air Fryer pan and cover with the pork pieces.
6. Air fry for about 15 minutes, flipping once halfway through.
7. Remove from air fryer and transfer the pork mixture onto serving plates.
8. Serve hot.

Per serving: Calories: 218Kcal; Fat: 8.8g; Protein: 27.7g; Carbohydrates: 7.1g; Sugar: 3.7g; Sodium: 110mg

86. Pork Tenderloin with Bacon & Veggies

Preparation time: 20 minutes

Cooking time: 28 minutes

Servings: 3

Ingredients:

- 3 potatoes
- ¾ pound frozen green beans
- 6 bacon slices
- 3: 6-ouncespork tenderloins
- 2 tablespoons olive oil

Directions:

1. Preheat the air fryer to 390°F and oil the air fryer basket.
2. With a fork, pierce the potatoes.
3. Place potatoes into the prepared air fryer basket and air fry for about 15 minutes.
4. Wrap one bacon slice around 4-6 green beans.
5. Coat the pork tenderloins with oil
6. After 15 minutes, add the pork tenderloins into air fryer basket with potatoes and air fry for about 5-6 minutes.
7. Remove the pork tenderloins from basket.
8. Place bean rolls into the basket and top with the pork tenderloins.
9. Air fry for another 7 minutes.
10. Remove from air fryer and transfer the pork tenderloins onto a platter.
11. Cut each tenderloin into desired size slices.
12. Serve alongside the potatoes and green beans rolls.

Per serving: Calories: 918Kcal; Fat: 47.7g; Protein: 77.9g; Carbohydrate: 42.4g; Sugar: 4g; Sodium: 1400mg

87. Pork Loin with Potatoes

Preparation time: 15 minutes

Cooking time: 25 minutes

Servings: 5

Ingredients:

- 2 pounds pork loin
- 3 tablespoons olive oil, divided
- 1 teaspoon fresh parsley, chopped
- Salt and ground black pepper, as required
- 3 large red potatoes, chopped
- ½ teaspoon garlic powder
- ½ teaspoon red pepper flakes, crushed

Directions:

1. Coat the pork loin with oil and then, season evenly with parsley, salt, and black pepper.
2. In a huge bowl, add the potatoes, remaining oil, garlic powder, red pepper flakes, salt, and black pepper then toss to coat well.
3. Set the temperature of air fryer to 325°F. Oil the air fryer basket.
4. Place loin into the prepared air fryer basket.
5. Arrange potato pieces around the pork loin.
6. Air fry for about 25 minutes.
7. Remove from air fryer and transfer the pork loin onto a platter, wait for about 5 minutes before slicing.
8. Cut the pork loin into desired size slices and serve alongside the potatoes.

Per serving: Calories: 556Kcal; Fat: 28.3g; Protein: 44.9g; Carbohydrate: 29.6g; Sugar: 1.9g; Sodium: 132mg

88. Pork Rolls

Preparation time: 20 minutes

Cooking time: 15 minutes

Servings: 4

Ingredients:

- 1 scallion, chopped
- ¼ cup sun-dried tomatoes, finely chopped
- 2 tablespoons fresh parsley, chopped
- Salt and ground black pepper, as required
- 4: 6-ouncespork cutlets, pounded slightly
- 2 teaspoons paprika
- ½ tablespoon olive oil

Directions:

1. In a bowl, mix well scallion, tomatoes, parsley, salt, and black pepper.
2. Spread the tomato mixture over each pork cutlet.
3. Roll each cutlet and secure with cocktail sticks.
4. Rub the outer part of rolls with paprika, salt, and black pepper.
5. Coat the rolls evenly with oil.
6. Set the temperature of air fryer to 390°F. Grease an air fryer basket.
7. Arrange pork rolls into the prepared air fryer basket in a single layer.
8. Air fry for about 15 minutes.
9. Remove from air fryer and transfer the pork rolls onto serving plates.
10. Serve hot.

Per serving: Calories: 244Kcal; Fat: 8.2g; Protein: 20.1g; Carbohydrate: 14.5g; Sugar: 1.7g; Sodium: 708mg

89. Pork Sausage Casserole

Preparation time: 15 minutes

Cooking time: 30 minutes

Servings: 4

Ingredients:

- 6 ounces flour, sifted
- 2 eggs
- 1 red onion, thinly sliced
- 1 garlic clove, minced
- Salt and ground black pepper, as required
- ¾ cup milk
- 2/3 cup cold water
- 8 small sausages
- 8 fresh rosemary sprigs

Directions:

1. In a bowl, combine the flour and the eggs.
2. Add the onion, garlic, salt, and pepper to the dish. Mix thoroughly.
3. Add the milk and water and mix until thoroughly combined.
4. Pierce one rosemary sprig into each link.
5. Adjust the air fryer's temperature to 320°F. Endeavor to oil the ovenproof dish.
6. Spread the flour mixture evenly over the top of the sausages in the prepared baking dish.
7. Air-fry for roughly thirty minutes.
8. Take the food out of the air fryer and serve warm.

Per serving: Calories: 334Kcal; Fat: 14g; Protein: 14g; Carbohydrate: 37.7g; Sugar: 3.5g; Sodium: 250mg

90. Juicy Lamb Chops

Preparation time: 10 minutes

Cooking time: 14 minutes

Servings: 4

Ingredients:

- 4 lamb chops
- 2 garlic cloves, minced
- 2 tbsp. of olive oil
- Pepper
- Salt

Directions:

1. Coat lamb chops with oil and rub with garlic, pepper, and salt.
2. Place the dehydrating tray in a multi-level Air Fryer basket and place the basket in the instant pot.
3. Place lamb chops on dehydrating tray.
4. Seal pot with Air Fryer lid and select air fry mode, then set the temperature to 350°F

and timer for 14 minutes. Turn lamb chops halfway through.

5. Serve and enjoy.

Per serving: Calories: 313Kcal; Fat: 16.9g; Protein: 38g; Carbohydrates: 0.5g; Sugar: 0g; Sodium: 350mg

91. Crispy Lamb

Preparation time: 10 minutes

Cooking time: 30 minutes

Servings: 4

Ingredients:

- 1 tablespoon breadcrumbs
- 2 tablespoons macadamia nuts, toasted and crushed
- 1 tablespoon olive oil
- 1 garlic clove, minced
- 28 ounces rack of lamb
- Salt and black pepper to the taste
- 1 egg
- 1 tablespoon rosemary, chopped

Directions:

1. In a bowl, mix oil with garlic and stir well.
2. Season lamb with salt, pepper, and brush with the oil.
3. In another bowl, mix nuts with breadcrumbs and rosemary.
4. Get a separate bowl and break egg. Whisk well.
5. Dip lamb in egg, then in macadamia mix, place them in your air fryer's basket, cook at 360 degrees F and cook for 25 minutes, increase heat to 400°F and cook for 5 minutes more.
6. Divide among plates and serve right away.
7. Enjoy!

Per serving: Calories: 230Kcal; Fat: 2g; Protein: 12g; Carbohydrates: 10g; Sugar: 2g; Sodium: 330mg

92. Lamb and Creamy Brussels Sprouts

Preparation time: 10 minutes

Cooking time: 1 hour and 10 minutes

Servings: 4

Ingredients:

- 2 pounds leg of lamb, scored
- 2 tablespoons olive oil
- 1 tablespoon rosemary, chopped
- 1 tablespoon lemon thyme, chopped
- 1 garlic clove, minced
- and 1/2-pounds Brussels sprouts, trimmed
- 1 tablespoon butter, melted
- 1/2 cup sour cream
- Salt and black pepper to the taste

Directions:

1. Season leg of lamb with salt, pepper, thyme, and rosemary, brush with oil, place in your air fryer's basket, cook at 300 degrees F for 1 hour, and transfer to a plate keep warm.
2. Using a pan for the air fryer, mix Brussels sprouts with salt, pepper, garlic, butter, and sour cream, toss, put in your air fryer and cook at 400°F for 10 minutes.
3. Divide lamb on plates, add Brussels sprouts on the side and serve.
4. Enjoy!

Per serving: Calories: 440Kcal; Fat: 23g; Protein: 49g; Carbohydrates: 2g; Sugar: 3g; Sodium: 280mg

93. Rosemary Lamb Chops

Preparation time: 30 minutes

Cooking time: 20 minutes

Servings: 2 to 3

Ingredients:

- 2 teaspoons oil
- ½ teaspoon ground rosemary
- ½ teaspoon lemon juice
- 1 pound (454 g) lamb chops, approximately 1-inch thick
- Salt and pepper to taste
- Cooking spray

Directions:

1. Mix the oil, rosemary, and lemon juice and rub into all sides of the lamb chops. Season to taste with salt and pepper.
2. For best flavor, cover lamb chops and allow them to rest in the fridge for 15 to 20 minutes.
3. Spray air fryer basket with nonstick spray and place lamb chops in it.
4. Air fry at 360°F (182°C) for approximately 20 minutes. This will cook chops to medium. The meat will be juicy but have no remaining pink. Air fry for 1 to 2 minutes longer for well-done chops. For rare chops, stop cooking after about 12 minutes and check for doneness.

Per serving: Calories: 237Kcal; Fat: 13g; Protein: 30g; Carbohydrates: 0g; Sugar: 0g; Sodium: 116mg

94. Hawaiian Chicken Packet

Preparation time: 15 minutes

Cooking time: 20 minutes

Servings: 4

Ingredients:

- 4 skinless, boneless chicken breast halves
- 1 green bell pepper, sliced into strips
- 1 onion, chopped
- 1 green bell pepper
- 1 cup of bottled teriyaki sauce or marinade
- 1 can of pineapple chunks, drained

Directions:

1. Preheat your air fryer to medium-high heat
2. Seeded and sliced bell pepper into strips
3. Spread aluminum foil on your countertop and place a piece of chicken in the center.
4. Coat the chicken with the teriyaki sauce by pouring the sauce on the chicken.
5. Sprinkle some pineapple chunks, onions, red peppers, and green peppers on the piece of chicken.
6. Fold the foil and seal it. Do the same to other pieces of chicken.
7. Cook them in your air fryer for 20 minutes. You may need to take one piece out to check its doneness before removing the other pieces of chicken.
8. You can now serve them.

Per serving: Calories: 304.1Kcal; Fat: 1.7g; Protein: 33g; Carbohydrates: 38.9g; Sugar: 1g; Sodium: 240mg

95. Turkey and Zucchini Burgers with Corn on the Cob

Preparation time: 15 minutes

Cooking time: 15 – 20 minutes

Servings: 4

Ingredients:

- 5 ounces of ground turkey breast
- 4 1/4-inch-thick slices of pepper Jack cheese (1 oz.)
- 3 tablespoons of panko breadcrumbs
- 3 tablespoons of finely chopped red or yellow onion
- 2 whole-wheat hamburger rolls, split and toasted
- 2 teaspoons of mayonnaise
- 2 teaspoons of low-fat plain yogurt
- 2 tablespoons of finely chopped jalapeño pepper
- 1 1/4 cups of thinly sliced red cabbage
- 1 tablespoon of lime juice
- 1 tablespoon and 1/2 teaspoon of canola oil
- 1 ear corn, husked and halved
- 3/4 teaspoon of chili powder
- 1/2 teaspoon of ground cumin
- 1/2 cup of shredded zucchini
- 1/4 teaspoon of salt
- 1/8 teaspoon of ground pepper

Directions:

1. Add 1/8 teaspoon of salt, 1 tablespoon of oil, lime juice, jalapeno, and cabbage together in a bowl. In another bowl, you should combine the chili powder with the yogurt and mayonnaise.
2. Brush the corn with 1/2 teaspoon of oil.
3. Add 1/8 teaspoon of salt with pepper, cumin, onion, panko, zucchini, and turkey. Marsh and the items together into a paste-like mixture.
4. Cook the corn for about 7 to 10 minutes. Also, you should heat the patties until they are browned. This should take about 5 minutes of continuous heating.
5. Top the patties with cheese slices before they are done. This will allow the cheese to melt.
6. Put mayonnaise mixture on the cut sides of the hamburger rolls.
7. Divide the remaining slaw on the rolls. Top the burger with the roll tops and the patties before cutting the corn into half.
8. Serve half corn with a whole burger.

Per serving: Calories: 446Kcal; Fat: 19g; Protein: 21g; Carbohydrates: 43g; Sugar: 2g; Sodium: 380mg

96. Long-Roasted Chicken Thighs

Preparation time: 10 minutes

Cooking time: 3 hours

Servings: 4

Ingredients:

- Kosher salt
- 8 skin-on, bone-in chicken thighs
- 4 cloves of garlic (should be sliced)
- 4 bay leaves, torn in half
- Black pepper

Directions:

1. Season the chicken a day or two before you cook this recipe.
2. Sprinkle some salt on both sides of the chicken thighs.
3. Mix the garlic, bay leaves, and black pepper together. Coat the chicken thighs in the mixture before you refrigerate them for at least 24 hours.
4. Preheat your air fryer and cook the chicken thighs at 350°F for up to 2 hours.
5. Reduce the heat to 325°F and cook it for another 1 hour. This will make the chicken thighs crispy, but they will also shrink in size. They will be golden brown.
6. You can now serve them with vegetable salad.

Per serving: Calories: 225Kcal; Fat: 14g;Protein: 20g; Carbohydrates: 3g; Sugar: 4g; Sodium: 440mg

97. Mini Turkey Meatballs

Preparation time: 15 minutes

Cooking time: 10 minutes

Servings: 5

Ingredients:

- 3 tablespoons of olive oil
- 3 tablespoons of ketchup
- 3 garlic cloves, minced
- 1/4 teaspoon of ground black pepper
- 1/4 cup of grated Pecorino Romano
- 1/4 cup of grated Parmesan
- 1/4 cup of dried breadcrumbs
- 1/4 cup of Italian parsley leaves, chopped
- 1 teaspoon of salt
- 1 small onion, grated
- 1 pound of ground dark turkey meat
- 1 large egg

Directions:

1. Get a big bowl. Add pepper, salt, Pecorino, Parmesan, parsley, ketchup, breadcrumbs, egg, garlic, and onion together.
2. Whisk them until they mix evenly. Add the turkey and mix them.
3. Shape the mixture into several meatballs. Air fry the meatballs for about 5 minutes. They should be brown by them.
4. Now prepare your favorite sauce and dredge the meatballs in it.
5. You can now serve the turkey meatballs. They are best served either warm or hot.

Per serving: Calories: 48Kcal; Fat: 10g;Protein: 3g; Carbohydrates: 3g; Sugar: 2g; Sodium: 270mg

98. White Chicken Chili

Preparation time: 10 minutes

Cooking time: 45 minutes

Servings: 4

Ingredients:

- 1 pound of boneless skinless chicken breasts (should be chopped)
- 1 medium onion (to be chopped)
- 1 tablespoon of olive oil
- 2 garlic cloves, minced

- 2 cans of chicken broth
- 1 can of chopped green chiles

Directions:

1. Cook both chicken and onion in oil until they are browned. Add the garlic before you cook the mixture a minute more.
2. Stir in cayenne, oregano, cumin, chiles, and the broth and boil them together.
3. Mash a can of beans until it becomes like a paste. Add it to a saucepan and add the remaining beans to the same saucepan.
4. Add the chicken to the beans and cook them at low heat for about 30 minutes or until the chicken changes its color from pink and the onion is tender.
5. You can now serve it with cheese and jalapeno pepper.

Per serving: Calories: 219Kcal; Fat: 7g;Protein: 19g; Carbohydrates: 21g; Sugar: 2g; Sodium: 310mg

99. Herbed Chicken Marsala

Preparation time: 10 minutes

Cooking time: 30 minutes

Servings: 4

Ingredients:

- Kosher salt and freshly ground black pepper
- 4-ounce boneless, skinless chicken breast cutlets
- 3/4 cup of low-sodium chicken broth
- 2 teaspoons of unsalted butter
- 2 tablespoons fresh flat-leaf parsley, roughly chopped
- 10 ounces of white button or cremini (baby Bella) mushrooms, sliced
- 1/3 cup of whole wheat flour
- 1/3 cup of sweet marsala wine

- 1/3 cup of sun-dried tomatoes (not packed in oil; not rehydrated), finely chopped or very thinly sliced
- 1/2 teaspoon of chopped fresh rosemary
- 1 1/2 tablespoon of extra-virgin olive oil

Directions:

1. Pound the chicken cutlets to flatten it. Sprinkle it with 1/4 teaspoon each of salt and pepper.
2. Coat the chicken with flour and air fry it for about 4 minutes. It should be golden brown by then. Place it in an airtight container to keep it warm.
3. After removing the chicken, add rosemary, sun-dried tomatoes, and 1/2 cup of the chicken broth to what is left in the fryer after the chicken is removed. Cook the mixture for a minute.
4. Mix the mushrooms with 1/2 teaspoon of pepper and 1/4 teaspoon of salt. Cook the mixture for 5 minutes to make the mushrooms soft.
5. Add marsala to the mushroom mixture and boil them together.
6. Add the remaining 1/4 cup of broth to the butter and cook them with low heat to melt the butter. This should not exceed 30 seconds.
7. Top the chicken with the sauce and mushroom mixture before you serve it. You should also sprinkle it with some parsley.

Per serving: Calories: 294Kcal; Fat: 11g; Protein: 30g; Carbohydrates: 19g; Sugar: 1g; Sodium: 250mg

100. Chicken Alfredo

Preparation time: 10 minutes

Cooking time: 25 – 30 minutes

Servings: 4

Ingredients:

- Some Kosher salt
- Freshly ground black pepper
- Freshly chopped parsley, for garnish
- 8 oz. of fettuccini
- 2 tablespoons of extra-virgin olive oil
- 2 cloves garlic, minced
- 2 boneless skinless chicken breasts
- 1/2 cup of heavy cream
- 1 cup of freshly grated Parmesan
- 1 1/2 cup of whole milk
- 1 1/2 cup of low-sodium chicken broth

Directions:

1. The first thing to do is to heat the olive oil.

2. Add the chicken, a pinch of salt, and pepper to the oil and cook it in your air fryer.

3. Cook it for about 8 minutes, which will make it turn crispy and golden.

4. Get the chicken and let it cool for 10 minutes before you slice it.

5. Mix the garlic with the milk and broth. Add pepper and salt to the mixture.

6. Stir fettuccine into the mixture. Cook it until it becomes thick and firm. This should not exceed 8 minutes.

7. Stir the parmesan and cream into the broth mixture. Leave it for some time to allow it to thicken.

8. Remove the broth from the air fryer and add your slices of chicken into it. Now, you can garnish it with parsley. That's all. You can now serve it.

Per serving: Calories: 310Kcal; Fat: 17g;Protein: 17g; Carbohydrates: 23g; Sugar: 3g; Sodium: 390mg

CHAPTER 6: Desserts

101. Spiced Apples

Preparation time: 5 minutes

Cooking time: 17 minutes

Servings: 4

Ingredients:

- 4 small apples, cored, sliced
- 2 tablespoons erythritol sweeteners
- 1 teaspoon apple pie spice
- 2 tablespoons olive oil

Directions:

1. Switch on your air fryer, insert fryer basket, grease it with olive oil, then shut with its lid, set the fryer at 350 degrees F, and preheat for 5 minutes.
2. Meanwhile, place apple slices in a bowl, sprinkle with sweetener and spice, and drizzle with oil and stir until evenly coated.
3. Open the fryer, add apple slices in it, close with its lid and cook for 12 minutes until nicely golden and crispy, shaking halfway through the frying.
4. Serve straight away.

Per serving: Calories: 89.6Kcal; Fat: 2g; Protein: 0.5g; Carbohydrates: 21.8g; Sugar: 1g; Sodium: 330mg

102. Chocolate Lava Cake

Preparation time: 5 minutes

Cooking time: 13 minutes

Servings: 2

Ingredients:

- 1 tablespoon flax meal
- 1/2 teaspoon baking powder
- 2 tablespoons cocoa powder, unsweetened
- 2 tablespoons erythritol sweeteners
- 1/8 teaspoon Stevia sweetener
- 1/8 teaspoon vanilla extract, unsweetened
- 1 tablespoon olive oil
- 2 tablespoons water
- 1 egg, pastured

Directions:

1. Switch on the air fryer, insert fryer basket, grease it with olive oil, then shut with its lid, set the fryer at 350 degrees F, and preheat for 5 minutes.
2. Meanwhile, take a two cups ramekin, grease it with oil and set aside.
3. Get a small bowl and put all ingredients. Mix until well combined and incorporated. Pour the batter into the ramekin.
4. Open the fryer, place ramekin in it, close with its lid and cook for 8 minutes until cake is done and inserted skewer into the cake slides out clean.
5. When air fryer beeps, open its lid, take out the ramekin and let the cake cool in it.
6. Then take out the cake, cut it into slices, and serve.

Per serving: Calories: 362.8Kcal; Fat: 33.6g; Protein: 11.7g; Carbohydrates: 3.4g; Sugar: 1g; Sodium: 450mg

103. Apple Crumble Jars

Preparation time: 15 minutes

Cooking time: 24 minutes

Servings: 6

Ingredients:

For Apple Filling

- 3 cups diced, peeled, seeded Granny Smith apples (approximately 3 large)
- tablespoon lemon juice
- 1 tablespoon gluten-free all-purpose flour
- 2 tablespoons light brown sugar
- 1/2 teaspoon ground cinnamon
- 1 tablespoon butter, melted
- 1/8 teaspoon salt
- 6 (4-ounce) glass jelly jars

For Crumble Topping

- 2 tablespoons gluten-free all-purpose flour
- 1/3 cup old-fashioned oats
- 1/4 cup chopped pecans
- 4 teaspoons light brown sugar
- 1/4 teaspoon ground cinnamon
- 1/8 teaspoon ground nutmeg
- 2 tablespoons butter, melted
- 1/8 teaspoon salt

Directions:

1. To make Apple Filling: Place diced apples in a medium bowl and toss with lemon juice. Add remaining filling ingredients and toss.
2. Ready air fryer at 350°F for 3 minutes.
3. Distribute apple mixture among jelly jars. Place three jars in the air fryer basket. Cook 7 minutes. Repeat with remaining jars.
4. To make Crumble Topping: While the apple mixture is cooking, combine Crumble Topping ingredients in a medium bowl.
5. Once the cooked put Crumble Topping. Bake for another 5 minutes in batches of three jars.
6. Let jars cool 10 minutes before covering. Refrigerate 'til ready to serve, up to 4 days.

Per serving: Calories: 250Kcal; Fat: 8g;Protein: 3g; Carbohydrates: 29g; Sugar: 2g; Sodium: 310mg

104. Kiwi Pavlova with Lemon Cream

Preparation time: 15 minutes

Cooking time: 90 minutes

Servings: 2

Ingredients:

For Pavlova

- 2 egg whites
- 1/4 teaspoon cornstarch
- 1/2 cup granulated sugar
- 1/2 teaspoon lemon juice
- 1/2 teaspoon vanilla extract

For Topping

- 1/3 cup heavy whipping cream
- 1 teaspoon lemon juice
- 1/4 teaspoon lemon zest
- 2 tablespoons granulated sugar
- 2 medium kiwis, peeled and sliced

Directions:

To make Pavlova:

1. Get a grill pan and cut a piece of parchment to the size of it. Make a circle (6 inches) on paper.
2. Turn the paper onto grill pan. You have to see circle outline. Set aside.
3. Get a large metal bowl. Prepare an electric mixer, set to high speed, and beat egg whites.

4. Add cornstarch while beating. Put 1 tbsp. of sugar at a time, 'til stiff peaks form in the mixture. Add lemon juice and vanilla.

5. Prepare the air fryer at 225°F for 5 minutes.

6. Put egg white mixture over parchment paper circle, creating higher edges around perimeter (like a short pie crust). Make an indention in center.

7. Arrange grill pan to fryer basket and cook 60 minutes.

8. Once cooked. Turn off heat and then, leave for 30 minutes.

9. Take the grill pan and slowly peel off parchment paper from the bottom of pavlova. Move the pavlova to a plate.

To make Topping:

10. Get a medium-sized bowl, whisk the whipping cream, lemon juice, lemon zest, and sugar together until is creamy.

11. Fill pavlova crust with whipped cream mixture and top with kiwi slices. Serve.

Per serving: Calories: 320Kcal; Fat: 13g;Protein: 4g; Carbohydrates: 40g; Sugar: 1g; Sodium: 150mg

105. Amaretto Cheesecake

Preparation time: 10 minutes

Cooking time: 22 minutes

Servings: 6

Ingredients:

For Crust

- 1/2 cup Corn Chex
- 2/3 cup blanched slivered almonds
- 1 tablespoon light brown sugar
- 3 tablespoons butter, melted

For Cheesecake

- 14 ounces cream cheese, room temperature
- 2 tablespoons sour cream

- 1 large egg
- 1/2 cup granulated sugar
- 1/2 cup Amaretto liqueur
- 1/2 teaspoon lemon juice
- 1/8 teaspoon salt

Directions:

1. To make Crust: Pulse Corn Chex, almonds, and brown sugar in a food processor until it has a powdered consistency.

2. Put into a small bowl and add melted butter. Combine with a fork until butter is well distributed. Press mixture into a 7" springform pan lightly greased with preferred cooking oil.

3. Preheat air fryer at 400°F for 3 minutes.

4. To make Cheesecake: Combine cream cheese, sour cream, egg, sugar, Amaretto, lemon juice, and salt in a large bowl. Spoon over crust. Cover with aluminum foil.

5. Place springform pan in air fryer basket and cook 16 minutes. Remove aluminum foil and cook an additional 6 minutes.

6. Remove cheesecake from air fryer basket. Cheesecake will be a little jiggly in center.

7. Cover and refrigerate at least 2 hours to allow it to set. Once set, release side pan, and serve.

Per serving: Calories: 280Kcal; Fat: 14g;Protein: 4g; Carbohydrates: 29g; Sugar: 5g; Sodium: 450mg

106. Lemon Cheesecake with Raspberry Sauce

Preparation time: 10 minutes

Cooking time: 22 minutes

Servings: 6

Ingredients:

For Crust

- 1 cup cornflakes cereal
- 2 tablespoons granulated sugar
- 4 tablespoons butter, melted

For Cheesecake

- 12 ounces cream cheese, room temperature
- 2 tablespoons sour cream
- 2 large eggs
- 1/2 cup granulated sugar
- 1 tablespoon lemon zest
- 1 tablespoon fresh lemon juice
- 1 teaspoon vanilla extract
- 1/8 teaspoon salt

For Raspberry Sauce

- 1 1/2 cups fresh raspberries
- 2 tablespoons lemon juice
- 1/2 cup granulated sugar

Directions:

1. To make Crust: Pulse together cornflakes, sugar, and butter in a food processor. Press mixture into a 7" springform pan lightly greased with preferred cooking oil.
2. Preheat air fryer at 400°F for 3 minutes.
3. To make Cheesecake: Combine cream cheese, sour cream, eggs, sugar, lemon zest, lemon juice, vanilla, and salt in a large bowl. Spoon into crust. Cover with aluminum foil.
4. Place springform pan in air fryer basket and cook 16 minutes. Remove aluminum foil and cook an additional 6 minutes.
5. To make Raspberry Sauce: While cheesecake is baking, add Raspberry Sauce ingredients to a small saucepan over medium heat and cook 5 minutes. Using back of a spoon, smoosh raspberries against side of saucepan while cooking. After berries are smooshed and sauce has thickened, pour through a sieve to filter out seeds. Refrigerate covered until ready to use.
6. Remove cheesecake from air fryer. Cheesecake will be a little jiggly in center. Cover and refrigerate at least 2 hours to allow it to set. Once set, release side pan, and serve with Raspberry Sauce poured over slices.

Per serving: Calories: 268Kcal; Fat: 8g; Protein: 12g; Carbohydrates: 35g; Sugar: 3g; Sodium: 250mg

107. Perfect Cinnamon Toast

Preparation time: 5 minutes

Cooking time: 5 – 10 minutes

Servings: 1

Ingredients:

- 2 tsp. pepper
- 1 1/2 tsp. vanilla extract
- 1 1/2 tsp. cinnamon
- 1/2 C. sweetener of choice
- 1 C. coconut oil
- 12 slices whole-wheat bread

Directions:

1. Melt coconut oil and mix with sweetener until dissolved. Mix in remaining ingredients minus bread till incorporated.
2. Spread mixture onto bread, covering all areas. Place coated pieces of bread in your air fryer.
3. Cook 5 minutes at 400°F.
4. Remove and cut diagonally. Enjoy!

Per serving: Calories: 124Kcal; Fat: 2g; Protein: 2g; Carbohydrates: 8g; Sugar: 17g; Sodium: 480mg

108. Apple Dumplings

Preparation time: 10 minutes

Cooking time: 25 minutes

Servings: 4

Ingredients:

- 2 tbsp. melted coconut oil
- 2 puff pastry sheets
- 1 tbsp. brown sugar
- 2 tbsp. raisins
- 2 small apples of choice

Directions:

1. Ensure your air fryer is preheated to 356°F.
2. Core and peel apples and mix with raisins and sugar.
3. Place a bit of apple mixture into puff pastry sheets and brush sides with melted coconut oil.
4. Place into air fryer. Cook for 25 minutes, turning halfway through. It will be golden when done.

Per serving: Calories: 260Kcal; Fat: 7g; Protein: 2g; Carbohydrates: 35g; Sugar: 11g; Sodium: 380mg

109. Easy Air Fryer Donuts

Preparation time: 10 minutes

Cooking time: 10 – 15 minutes

Servings: 8

Ingredients:

- Pinch of allspice
- 4 tbsp. dark brown sugar
- 1/2 - 1 tsp. cinnamon
- 1/3 C. granulated sweetener
- 3 tbsp. melted coconut oil
- 1 can of biscuits

Directions:

1. Mix allspice, sugar, sweetener, and cinnamon.
2. Take out biscuits from the can and with a circle cookie cutter, cut holes from centers, and place into the air fryer.
3. Cook 5 minutes at 350°F. As batches are cooked, use a brush to coat with melted coconut oil and dip each into a sugar mixture.
4. Serve warm!

Per serving: Calories: 209Kcal; Fat: 4g; Protein: 5g; Carbohydrates: 39g; Sugar: 12g; Sodium: 280mg

110. Chocolate Soufflé

Preparation time: 10 minutes

Cooking time: 15 minutes

Servings: 2

Ingredients:

- 2 tbsp. almond flour
- 1/2 tsp. vanilla
- 3 tbsp. sweetener
- 2 separated eggs
- 1/4 C. melted coconut oil
- 3 ounces of semi-sweet chocolate, chopped

Directions:

1. Brush coconut oil and sweetener onto ramekins.
2. Melt coconut oil and chocolate together.
3. Beat egg yolks well, adding vanilla and sweetener. Stir in flour and ensure there are no lumps.
4. Preheat fryer to 330 °F.
5. Whisk egg whites till they reach peak state and fold them into chocolate mixture.
6. Pour butter into ramekins and place into the fryer.

7. Cook for 14 minutes.
8. Serve with powdered sugar. Sprinkle the sugar on it.

Per serving: Calories: 238Kcal; Fat: 6g; Protein: 1g; Carbohydrates: 23g; Sugar: 10g; Sodium: 460mg

111. Apple Hand Pies

Preparation time: 10 minutes

Cooking time: 10 minutes

Servings: 6

Ingredients:

- 15-ounces no-sugar-added apple pie filling
- 1 store-bought crust

Directions:

1. Layout pie crust and slice into equal-sized squares.
2. Place 2 tbsp. Filling into each square and seal crust with a fork.
3. Place into the fryer. Cook 8 minutes at 390°F until golden in color.

Per serving: Calories: 278Kcal; Fat: 10g; Protein: 5g; Carbohydrates: 23g; Sugar: 14g; Sodium: 342mg

112. Blueberry Lemon Muffins

Preparation time: 10 minutes

Cooking time: 10 minutes

Servings: 12

Ingredients:

- 1 tsp. vanilla
- Juice and zest of 1 lemon
- 2 eggs
- 1 C. blueberries
- 1/2 C. cream
- 1/4 C. avocado oil
- 1/2 C. monk fruit
- 2 1/2 C. almond flour

Directions:

1. Mix monk fruit and flour.
2. In another bowl, mix vanilla, egg, lemon juice, and cream.
3. Add mixtures together and blend well.
4. Spoon batter into cupcake holders. Place in an air fryer. Bake for 10 minutes at 320°F, check at 6 minutes to ensure you don't overbake them.

Per serving: Calories: 317Kcal; Fat: 11g; Protein: 3g; Carbohydrates: 31g; Sugar: 7g; Sodium: 543g

113. Pecan Pie Bread Pudding

Preparation time: 10 minutes

Cooking time: 15 minutes

Servings: 4

Ingredients:

- 2 cups (1") cubes gluten-free sandwich bread
- 1/2 cup pecan pieces
- 3 large eggs
- 1/4 cup half-and-half
- 1/4 cup dark corn syrup
- 1 teaspoon vanilla extract
- 2 tablespoons dark brown sugar
- 1/4 teaspoon ground cinnamon
- 1/4 teaspoon salt

Directions:

1. Place bread pieces in an ungreased 7" square cake barrel and spread pecan pieces evenly over the top.
2. In a medium bowl, whisk eggs. Stir in remaining ingredients.
3. Pour egg mixture over bread and pecans in cake barrel. Allow to cool for 10 minutes.
4. Preheat air fryer at 325°F for 3 minutes.
5. Place cake pan in the air fryer basket. Cook 15 minutes.

6. Transfer the pan to a cooling rack for 10 minutes. Once cooled slightly, slice and serve warm.

Per serving: Calories: 290Kcal; Fat: 25g;Protein: 3g; Carbohydrates: 16g; Sugar: 13g; Sodium: 264mg

114. Pumpkin Crunch Cake

Preparation time: 15 minutes

Cooking time: 35 minutes

Servings: 6

Ingredients:

For Crunch Layer

- 1/3 cup pecan pieces
- 5 gluten-free gingersnap cookies
- 1/3 cup light brown sugar
- 3 tablespoons butter, melted

For Cake

- 3 large eggs
- 3 tablespoons butter, melted
- 1/2 teaspoon vanilla extract
- 1 cup pumpkin purée
- 2 tablespoons sour cream
- 1/2 cup gluten-free all-purpose flour
- 1/4 cup tapioca flour
- 1/2 teaspoon xanthan gum
- 1/2 cup granulated sugar
- 1/2 teaspoon baking soda
- 1 teaspoon baking powder
- 1 teaspoon pumpkin pie spice
- 1/8 teaspoon salt

For Cream Cheese Frosting

- 6 ounces cream cheese, room temperature
- 11/3 cups powdered sugar
- 1/2 teaspoon vanilla extract
- 2 tablespoons butter, room temperature
- 1 tablespoon whole milk

Directions:

1. Place parchment paper in a pan. Put preferred cooking oil in paper and sides of the pan lightly.
2. To make Crunch Layer: In a food processor, pulse Crunch Layer ingredients until combined. Press mixture into the bottom of the cake pan.
3. To make Cake: Whisk together wet cake ingredients in a medium bowl. In a large bowl, sift together dry cake ingredients.
4. Warm air fryer at 350°F for 3 minutes.
5. Put wet ingredients to dry ingredients and gently combine. Do not overmix. Pour mixture into a cake pan. Cover with aluminum foil.
6. Place cake pan in the air fryer basket. Cook 30 minutes. Remove foil. Cook an additional 5 minutes.
7. Transfer cake pan to a cooling rack to cool 10 minutes. Once cooled, flip the cake onto a large serving platter.
8. To make Cream Cheese Frosting: Cream together frosting ingredients in a small bowl. Spread over cooled cake. Slice and serve.

Per serving: Calories: 253Kcal; Fat: 14g;Protein: 4g; Carbohydrates: 29g; Sugar: 15g; Sodium: 435mg

115. Carrot Cake Cupcakes

Preparation time: 10 minutes

Cooking time: 14 minutes

Servings: 8

Ingredients:

For Cupcakes

- 1 cup gluten-free all-purpose flour
- 1/2 teaspoon baking soda
- 1/3 cup light brown sugar

- 1/4 teaspoon salt
- 1/4 teaspoon ground cinnamon
- 1/8 teaspoon ground ginger
- 1 teaspoon vanilla extract
- 1 large egg
- 1 tablespoon buttermilk
- 1 tablespoon vegetable oil
- 1/4 cup grated carrots
- 2 tablespoons coconut shreds

For Cream Cheese Frosting

- 6 ounces cream cheese, room temperature
- 11/3 cups powdered sugar
- 1/2 teaspoon vanilla extract
- 2 tablespoons butter, room temperature
- 1 tablespoon whole milk
- 1/2 cup chopped walnuts

Directions:

1. To make Cupcakes: In a large bowl, combine flour, baking soda, sugar, salt, cinnamon, ginger, and vanilla. In your medium bowl, combine egg, buttermilk, oil, carrots, and coconut.
2. Preheat air fryer at 375°F for 3 minutes.
3. Pour wet ingredients from a medium-sized bowl into a large bowl with dry ingredients. Gently mix them together. Do not overmix. Spoon mixture into eight silicone cupcake liners lightly greased with preferred cooking oil.
4. Place four cupcake liners in an air fryer basket. Cook for 7 minutes.
5. Transfer cooked cupcakes to a cooling rack and let sit for 15 minutes. Repeat with remaining cupcakes.
6. To make Cream Cheese Frosting: In a mini bowl, beat cream cheese, sugar, vanilla, butter, and milk until smooth.

7. Spread frosting on cooled cupcakes. Sprinkle tops with chopped walnuts. Serve.

Per serving: Calories: 143Kcal; Fat: 1.9g;Protein: 6g; Carbohydrates: 24g; Sugar: 13g; Sodium: 827mg

116. Sweet Cream Cheese Wontons

Preparation time: 10 minutes
Cooking time: 10 minutes
Servings: 16
Ingredients:

- 1 egg mixed with a bit of water
- Wonton wrappers
- 1/2 C. powdered erythritol
- 8 ounces softened cream cheese
- Olive oil

Directions:

1. Mix sweetener and cream cheese together.
2. Layout 4 wontons at a time and cover with a dish towel to prevent drying out.
3. Place 1/2 of a teaspoon of cream cheese mixture into each wrapper.
4. Dip finger into egg/water mixture and fold diagonally to form a triangle. Seal edges well.
5. Repeat with remaining ingredients.
6. Place filled wontons into the air fryer and cook for 5 minutes at 400°F degrees F, shaking halfway through cooking.

Per serving: Calories: 188Kcal; Fat: 3g; Protein: 4g; arbohydrates: 27g; Sugar: 11g; Sodium: 634mg

117. Cinnamon Rolls

Preparation time: 1 hour

Cooking time: 15 minutes

Servings: 8

Ingredients:

- 1 1/2 tbsp. cinnamon
- 3/4 C. brown sugar
- 1/4 C. melted coconut oil
- 1-pound frozen bread dough, thawed

Glaze:

- 1/2 tsp. vanilla
- 1 1/4 C. powdered erythritol
- 2 tbsp. softened ghee
- 4 ounces softened cream cheese

Directions:

1. Layout bread dough and roll it out into a rectangle. Brush melted ghee over the dough and leave a 1-inch border along the edges.
2. Mix cinnamon and sweetener and then sprinkle over dough.
3. Roll dough tightly and slice into 8 pieces. Allow it to cool for 1-2 hours, so that it can rise.
4. To make the glaze, mix ingredients till smooth.
5. Once rolls rise, place into the air fryer and cook for 5 minutes at 350°F.
6. Serve rolls drizzled in cream cheese glaze. Enjoy!

Per serving: Calories: 234Kcal; Fat: 7g; Protein: 3g; Carbohydrates: 39g; Sugar: 11g; Sodium: 620mg

118. Baked Apple

Preparation time: 10 minutes

Cooking time: 10 minutes

Servings: 4

Ingredients:

- 1/4 C. water
- 1/4 tsp. nutmeg
- 1/4 tsp. cinnamon
- 1 1/2 tsp. melted ghee
- 2 tbsp. raisins
- 2 tbsp. chopped walnuts
- 1 medium apple

Directions:

1. Preheat your air fryer to 350°F.
2. Slice an apple in half and discard some of the flesh from the center.
3. Place into a frying pan.
4. Mix remaining ingredients together except water. Spoon mixture to the middle of apple halves.
5. Pour water overfilled apples.
6. Place pan with apple halves into the air fryer, bake for 20 minutes.

Per serving: Calories: 199Kcal; Fat: 9g; Protein: 1g; Carbohydrates: 17g; Sugar: 11g; Sodium: 620mg

119. Cinnamon Sugar Roasted Chickpeas

Preparation time: 10 minutes

Cooking time: 10 minutes

Servings: 2

Ingredients:

- 1 tbsp. sweetener
- 1 tbsp. cinnamon
- 1 C. chickpeas

Directions:

1. Preheat the air fryer to 390°F.
2. Rinse and drain chickpeas.
3. Mix all ingredients and add to the air fryer.
4. Cook 10 minutes.

Per serving: Calories: 111Kcal; Fat: 4g; Protein: 4g; Carbohydrates: 16g; Sugar: 10g; Sodium: 250mg

120. Cinnamon Fried Bananas

Preparation time: 10 minutes

Cooking time: 13 minutes

Servings: 2

Ingredients:

- 1 C. panko breadcrumbs
- 3 tbsp. cinnamon
- 1/2 C. almond flour
- 3 egg whites
- 8 ripe bananas
- 3 tbsp. vegan coconut oil

Directions:

1. Heat coconut oil and add breadcrumbs. Mix around 2-3 minutes until golden. Pour into a bowl.
2. Peel and cut bananas in half. Roll the half of each banana into flour, eggs, and crumb mixture. Place into the air fryer.
3. Cook for 10 minutes at 280°F
4. A great addition to a healthy banana split!

Per serving: Calories: 107Kcal; Fat: 0.7g; Protein: 1g; Carbohydrates: 27g; Sugar: 8g; Sodium: 430mg

CHAPTER 7: 30 Days Meal Plan

Days	Breakfast	Lunch	Dinner	Dessert
1	Shrimp Rice Frittata **Error! Bookmark not defined.**	Rosemary Lamb Chops	Fish Taco	Cinnamon Fried Bananas
2	Almond Crunch Granola **Error! Bookmark not defined.**	Buckwheat And Potato Flat Bread	Lamb And Creamy Brussels Sprouts	Amaretto Cheesecake
3	Mixed Berry Dutch Pancake	Mexican-Style Brown Rice Casserole	Savory Cheesy Cornmeal Biscuits	Lemon Cheesecake With Raspberry Sauce
4	Yogurt Raspberry Cake	Pork Tenderloin With Bacon & Veggies	Cheese And Bacon Crescent Ring	Chocolate Lava Cake
5	Egg-In-A-Hole	Japanese Chicken And Rice Salad	Italian Beef Meatballs	Apple Hand Pies
6	Spinach And Tomato Egg Cup	Steamer Clams	Juicy Lamb Chops	Apple Crumble Jars
7	Vegetable Frittata	Pork Tenderloin With Bell Peppers	Cheesy Lemon Halibut	Perfect Cinnamon Toast
8	Zucchini Bread	Colored Veggie Rice	Simply Shrimp	Spiced Apples
9	Spinach And Tomato Frittata	Smoky Fried Calamari	Delicious Coconut Granola	Pumpkin Crunch Cake
10	Mushroom And Black Bean Burrito	Risotto Balls With Bacon And Corn	Beef And Veggie Spring Rolls	Baked Apple
11	Crunchy Fried French Toast Sticks	Crispy Lamb	Fried Green Beans With Pecorino Romano	Cinnamon Rolls

12	Egg And Cheese Pockets	Classic Lobster Salad	Easy Rosemary Green Beans	Cinnamon Sugar Roasted Chickpeas
13	Egg Muffins With Bell Pepper	Roasted Chickpeas	Long-Roasted Chicken Thighs	Carrot Cake Cupcakes
14	Pancakes	Seafood Fritters	Saltine Wax Beans	Chocolate Soufflé
15	Bacon And Egg Sandwiches	White Chicken Chili	Asian-Style Shrimp Pilaf	Blueberry Lemon Muffins
16	Egg And Avocado Breakfast Burrito	Lemony Green Beans	Baked Avocados With Smoked Salmon	Apple Crumble Jars
17	Pumpkin Oatmeal With Raisins	Air Fryer Risotto Balls	Chicken Alfredo	Perfect Cinnamon Toast
18	Herb Frittata	Herbed Chicken Marsala	Tuna Melts On Tomatoes	Spiced Apples
19	Scotch Eggs	Shrimp Spring Rolls With Sweet Chili Sauce	Green Beans	Pumpkin Crunch Cake
20	Huevos Rancheros	Breaded Fish Sticks With Tartar Sauce	Juicy Lamb Chops	Baked Apple
21	Mixed Berry Dutch Pancake	Pork Rolls	Cheesy Lemon Halibut	Cinnamon Rolls
22	Yogurt Raspberry Cake	Bay Scallops	Sage Beef	Cinnamon Fried Bananas
23	Egg-In-A-Hole	Spicy Seafood Risotto	Bacon-Wrapped Stuffed Shrimp	Amaretto Cheesecake
24	Spinach And Tomato Egg Cup	Beef Pot Pie	Crab Cakes With Arugula And Blackberry Salad	Lemon Cheesecake With Raspberry Sauce
25	Vegetable Frittata	Thyme Scallops	Chili Lime–Crusted Halibut	Chocolate Lava Cake
26	Zucchini Bread	Gambas With Sweet Potato	Pork Sausage Casserole	Apple Hand Pies
27	Egg And Cheese Pockets	Tuna Croquettes	Paella-Style Spanish Rice	Kiwi Pavlova With Lemon Cream
28	Egg Muffins With Bell Pepper	Hawaiian Chicken Packet	Avocado Shrimp	Easy Air Fryer Donuts

29	Pancakes	Wild Rice Pilaf	Mini Turkey Meatballs	Pecan Pie Bread Pudding
30	Bacon And Egg Sandwiches	Pork Loin With Potatoes	Breaded Cod Sticks	Apple Dumplings

CHAPTER 8: Air Fryer Cook Times and Temperatures

It is essential to read your manufacturer's time and temperature instructions in order to have a good cooking experience. You can then adjust the time and temperature to fit the recipe you are making. This will help you ensure that you have well-cooked meals. Also, work with a food thermometer to arrive at the accurate internal temperature of meats and seafood for safe consumption.

Vegetables

	Temp (°F)	Time (mins)		Temp (°F)	Time (mins)
Asparagus (1-inch slices)	400 °F	5	Onions (quartered)	400 °F	11
Beets (whole)	400 °F	40	Parsnips (½-inch chunks)	380 °F	15
Bell Peppers (1-inch chunks)	400 °F	15	Pearl Onions	400 °F	10
Broccoli (florets)	400 °F	6	Potatoes (whole baby pieces)	400 °F	15
Broccoli Rabe (chopped)	400 °F	6	Potatoes (1-inch chunks)	400 °F	12
Brussel Sprouts (halved)	380 °F	15	Potatoes (baked whole)	400 °F	40
Cabbage (diced)	380 °F	15	Pumpkin (½-inch chunks)	380 °F	13
Carrots (halved)	380 °F	15	**Radishes**	380 °F	15
Cauliflower (florets)	400 °F	12	Squash (½-inch chunks)	400 °F	12
Collard Greens	250 °F	12	Sweet Potato (baked)	380 °F	30 to 35
Corn on the cob	390 °F	6	Tomatoes (halves)	350 °F	10
Cucumber (½-inch slices)	370 °F	4	Tomatoes (cherry)	400 °F	4
Eggplant (2-inch cubes)	400 °F	15	Turnips (½-inch chunks)	380 °F	15
Fennel (quartered)	370 °F	15	Zucchini (½-inch sticks)	400 °F	12
Green Beans	400 °F	5	Mushrooms (¼-inch slices)	400 °F	5
Kale (halved)	250 °F	12			

Chicken

	Temp (°F)	Time (mins)		Temp (°F)	Time (mins)
Breasts, bone in (1 ¼ lb.)	370 °F	25	Legs, bone-in (1 ¾ lb.)	380 °F	30
Breasts, boneless (4 oz)	380 °F	12	Thighs, boneless (1 ½ lb.)	380 °F	18 to 20
Drumsticks (2 ½ lb.)	370 °F	20	Wings (2 lb.)	400 °F	12
Game Hen (halved 2 lb.)	390 °F	20	Whole Chicken	360 °F	75
Thighs, bone-in (2 lb.)	380 °F	22	**Tenders**	360 °F	8 to 10

Beef

	Temp (°F)	Time (mins)		Temp (°F)	Time (mins)
Beef Eye Round Roast (4 lbs.)	400 °F	45 to 55	Meatballs (1-inch)	370 °F	7
Burger Patty (4 oz.)	370 °F	16 to 20	Meatballs (3-inch)	380 °F	10
Filet Mignon (8 oz.)	400 °F	18	Ribeye, bone-in (1-inch, 8 oz)	400 °F	10 to 15
Flank Steak (1.5 lbs.)	400 °F	12	Sirloin steaks (1-inch, 12 oz)	400 °F	9 to 14
Flank Steak (2 lbs.)	400 °F	20 to 28			

Pork & Lamb

	Temp (°F)	Time (mins)		Temp (°F)	Time (mins)
Bacon (regular)	400 °F	5 to 7	Pork Tenderloin	370 °F	15
Bacon (thick cut)	400 °F	6 to 10	**Sausages**	380 °F	15
Pork Loin (2 lb.)	360 °F	55	Lamb Loin Chops (1-inch thick)	400 °F	8 to 12
Pork Chops, bone in (1-inch, 6.5 oz)	400 °F	12	Rack of Lamb (1.5 – 2 lb.)	380 °F	22

Fish & Seafood

	Temp (°F)	Time (mins)		Temp (°F)	Time (mins)
Calamari (8 oz)	400 °F	4	Tuna Steak	400 °F	7 to 10
Fish Fillet (1-inch, 8 oz)	400 °F	10	**Scallops**	400 °F	5 to 7
Salmon, fillet (6 oz)	380 °F	12	**Shrimp**	400 °F	5
Swordfish steak	400 °F	10			

Frozen Foods

	Temp (°F)	Time (mins)		Temp (°F)	Time (mins)
Breaded Shrimp	400 °F	9	French Fries (thick - 17 oz)	400 °F	18
Chicken Nuggets (12 oz)	400 °F	10	Mozzarella Sticks (11 oz)	400 °F	8
Fish Sticks (10 oz.)	400 °F	10	Onion Rings (12 oz)	400 °F	8
Fish Fillets (½-inch, 10 oz)	400 °F	14	Pot Stickers (10 oz)	400 °F	8
French Fries (thin - 20 oz)	400 °F	14			

Converting Recipes

Take your favorite traditional method recipes and convert them to amazing air frying methods.. The fact is that you can air fry virtually anything you have as recipes rather than using an oven to prepare them. Remember, the air fryer heat is significantly intense than a standard oven. Therefore, start by reducing the suggested temperature by 25˚F to 50˚F and reduce the time by approximately 20%.

If the recipe calls for something to be baked at 425˚F for 60 minutes, you would air fry it at 400˚F for 48 minutes (although timing may vary). Always feel free to open the air fryer and check whether your meal or food is done or not..

Cooking packaged foods can also apply to the same rules as above. For example, if you are cooking frozen fries where the maker's cooking procedure suggests 450˚F for 18 minutes; then cook the fries at 400˚F for 15 minutes. Remember to shake the basket with items like French fries to help with the cooking process and to obtain even browning.

Index

Conclusion

Diabetes is a chronic disease that is becoming more rampant in our society by the day. These rising cases greatly affect our society and ameliorating it is non-negotiable.

Knowing how to control diabetes is very important to stay healthy and without having to worry about complications or sudden health problems. Thus, one significant way to control diabetes is to understand how much your diet can affect your blood sugar levels. There are small things you can do in the kitchen that can not only help with managing your diabetes but also benefit your overall health.

Cooking your food using an Air Fryer is an important kitchen secret that may help prevent diabetes. It can also improve the quality of your health positively. Air Fryers allow you to fry your food without all of the side effects that come along with frying with oil or deep frying.

The Air Fryer is not a solution to diabetes, but it offers a bunch of benefits that can help prevent the consumption of calories and fats that often propel diabetes. Using air fryers is one step towards living a healthy and balanced lifestyle.

This book is not only for those with diabetes but for every member of the family who desires to enjoy healthy and nutritious meals. This book encourages you to be positive, pay attention to your diet, and enjoy a great life. By following the cooking instructions and procedures presented in this book, I can assure you of a healthy lifestyle.

50382695R10044